ADEWALE MAJA-PEARCE was born in London in 1953. He grew up in Lagos, Nigeria, but returned to London to complete his education and gained a Master of Arts degree in African Studies at the School of Oriental and African Studies. He has held various positions in the literary world, is presently Africa Editor of the journal *Index on Censorship*, and also Series Editor of the African Writers Series.

His literary achievements include a collection of short stories about Nigeria, *Loyalties and Other Stories* (Longman, 1987); a travelogue, *In My Father's Country* (William Heinemann, 1987); and the scholarly poetry anthology, *Okigbo: Collected Poems* (Heinemann, 1986) which Maja-Pearce edited. His most recent works are *How Many Miles to Babylon?* (William Heinemann, 1990) and *Who's Afraid of Wole Soyinka?* (Heinemann, 1991).

D0609641

.H45 1990
emann book of
242011

OKANAGAN UNIVERSITY COLLEGE
LIBRARY
BRITISH COLUMBIA

OKANAGAN UNIV/COLLEGE LIBRARY

02420115

THE HEINEMANN BOOK OF AFRICAN POETRY IN ENGLISH

Selected by Adewale Maja-Pearce

HEINEMANN

Heinemann Educational Publishers
A division of Heinemann Publishers (Oxford) Ltd
Halley Court, Jordan Hill, Oxford OX2 8EJ

Heinemann: A division of Reed Publishing (USA) Inc.
361 Hanover Street, Portsmouth, NH 03801-3912, USA

Heinemann Educational Books (Nigeria) Ltd
PMB 5205, Ibadan
Heinemann Educational Boleswa
PO Box 10103, Village Post Office, Gaborone, Botswana

FLORENCE   PRAGUE   PARIS   MADRID
ATHENS   MELBOURNE   JOHANNESBURG
AUCKLAND   SINGAPORE   TOKYO
CHICAGO   SAO PAULO

© Introduction, Selection and Biographical Notes
Adewale Maja-Pearce 1990
First published by Heinemann International in the
African Writers Series in 1990

AFRICAN WRITERS SERIES and CARIBBEAN WRITERS SERIES and their
accompanying logos are trademarks in the United States of America of
Heinemann: A division of Reed Publishing (USA) Inc.

British Library Cataloguing in Publication Data
The Heinemann book of African poetry in English –
(African Writers Series)
1. Poetry in English. African writers, 1960 – Anthologies
I. Maja-Pearce, Adewale
821

ISBN 0-435-91323-9

Photoset by Wilmaset, Birkenhead, Wirral
Printed and bound in Great Britain by
Cox & Wyman Ltd, Reading, Berkshire

94 95 96 10 9 8 7 6 5 4

CONTENTS

Chenjerai Hove   *Zimbabwe, 1956*

Gabriel Gbadamosi   *Ireland/Nigeria, 1961*

ACKNOWLEDGEMENTS

The editor and publishers would like to thank the following for their permission to use copyright material: Catherine Obianuju Acholonu for Other Forms of Slaughter and Nigeria in the year 1999; Kofi Awoonor for Songs of Sorrow, The Weaver Bird, America, Long Island Sketches x, Songs of Abuse ii, Hymns of Praise, Celebration and Prayer ii, Afro-American Beats iii and The First Circle; Dennis Brutus for Their Behaviour, Postscripts 2, A Simple Lust is all my Woe, Sometimes a mesh of ideas, Nightsong: City, The Sounds begin again, Robben Island Sequence and For My Sons and Daughters; Syl Cheney-Coker for Letter to a Tormented Playwright, On Being a Poet in Sierra Leone and The Outsider; Steve Chimombo for The Messengers, Obituary, Of Promises and Prophecy, Four Ways of Dying, Derailment: A Delirium and A Death Song; Frank Chipasula for Manifesto on Ars Poetica (*Paper Air*, Vol 4, No 2, 1989); Frank Chipasula and Paul Green Publishers, Peterborough, for Dusk from *NIGHTWATCHER*, *Nightsong* which was published as the first booklet in the *Dangerous Writers* Series (Peterborough: Paul Green, 1986); Frank Chipasula and Raven Press, Johannesburg for A Love Poem for My Country (*New Classic*, 1978), Talking of Sharp Things and Friend, Ah you have changed! (*Staffrider*, Vol 5, No 2, 1982), Going Back Patiently (*ODI* Vol 1, No 2, March 1973), Ritual Girl, My Blood Brother, Those Rainy Mornings, Because the Wind Remembers, My Friendly People from *O Earth Wait for Me* (Johannesburg: Raven Press, 1984), and Tramp (*Cencrastus*, No 9, Summer 1982); J P Clark Bekederemo for Abiku, The Casualties, Epilogue to Casualties, The News from Ethiopia and the Sudan, A Family Procession, Death of a Lady, The Order of the Dead; The Estate of Christopher Okigbo for Poems Prophesying War, Thunder Can Break, Come Thunder, Hurrah for Thunder, Elegy for Slit-Drum, Elegy for Alto; Chenjerai Hove for Red Hills of Home, You Will Forget, Lost Bird, Migratory Bird 1, Child's Parliament, The Other Syllabus, Country Life; Gabriel Gbadamosi for The Reading, Death of the Polar Explorers, From: Sango; Kojo Laing for Senior lady sells garden eggs, Godhorse, Africa Sky, Tatale Swine, I am the freshly dead husband, The same corpse, Many worlds are walked at once, One hundred lines for the coast, Race on gathering bites, The huge car with the sad voice; Marjorie Oludhe Macgoye for Omera, August the First: The Watchman Speaks, August the First: The Shadow. Patel Speaks, August the First: Court Martial. The Mother Speaks; Marjorie Oludhe Macgoye and *London Magazine* for Mathenge (*London Magazine*, Vol 24, No 8, November 1984); Lupenga Mphande for Why the Old Woman Limps and the wood-cutter; The University of South Africa for Arthur Nortje's: Letter from Pretoria Central Prison, Newcombe at the Croydon Gallery, Waiting, Autopsy, Asservertions, Native's Letter, At Lansdowne Bridge, Cosmos in London; Odia Ofeimun for Prologue, How Can I Sing, Let Them Choose Paths, The Poet Lied, A Naming Day, A Handle for the Flutist, Beyond Fear I & II and Judgement Day from *The Poet Lied* (Lagos: Update Communications, 1988); Molara Ogundipe-Leslie for song of the African middle-class and On Reading an Archaeological Article; Tanure Ojaide for When Tomorrow is too long and Ward 6 from *The Fate of Vultures & Other Poems* (Oxford: Heinemann, 1989), What They Said from *Verdicts* and Launching Our Community Development Fund from *The Eagles Vision* (Detroit: Lotus Press, 1987); Niyi Osundare for Excursion, Who says that drought was here?, eyeful glances, Our Earth Will Not Die, Moonsongs iii, v, xviii, xix, and Goree; Lenrie Peters for The Present reigned supreme, Isatou died, and I am asking about the way ahead; Wole Soyinka for Fado Singer, Ogun Abibiman 1. Induction, After the Deluge, Apologia (Nkomati), and 'No!' He Said; Landeg White, for and on behalf of Jack Mapanje, for Messages, The Cheerful Girls at Smiller's Bar, 1971, These Too Are Our Elders, On African Writing, 1971, From Florrie Abraham Witness, December 1972, Glory Be to Chingwe's Hole, Making Our Clowns Martyrs, We Wondered About the Mellow Peaches, Another Fools' Day touches down: shush; Musaemura B. Zimunya and Longman, Zimbabwe for Arrivants and Kisimiso.

The publishers have made every effort to trace copyright holders, but in some cases without success. We shall be very glad to hear from anyone who has been inadvertently overlooked or incorrectly cited and make the necessary changes at the first opportunity.

INTRODUCTION

This anthology aims to represent the best African poetry written in English over the last thirty years. Unlike previous anthologies, it does not include translations from other languages, nor does it pretend to be comprehensive either in terms of one particular country or of the continent as a whole. Excellence has been the only criterion in making the selection, which is why some poets have been given more space than others, and why entire countries have been omitted altogether. The poets themselves are arranged in chronological order to give the reader a sense of the development of what used to be known as an 'emergent' tradition but which, on even a cursory reading of the more recent voices, has indisputably arrived.

Implicit in this anthology is the assumption that English is one of the languages of Africa. This is said against the background of a fierce debate which has been raging in African literary circles since Obi Wali published his famous article, 'The Dead End of African Literature?' in *Transition* in 1963: '. . . until these writers and their Western midwives accept the fact that any true African literature must be written in African languages, they would merely be pursuing a dead end which can only lead to sterility, uncreativity and frustration.' Obi Wali's statement has since been extended and refined by other African writers, most notably Ngũgĩ wa Thiong'o, the Kenyan novelist. In *Decolonising the Mind: The Politics of Language in African Literature* ('my farewell to English as a vehicle for any of my writings'), he argues that the continued use of the European languages merely perpetuates the colonial dependency which has brought the continent to the present point of collapse. An alternative vision of the African world, a pre-requisite for true liberation, can only be achieved through the medium of those languages which contain the 'collective experience' of the African people.

Ngũgĩ's argument is seductive, not least because it celebrates the cultural heritage of a continent that has suffered four centuries of denigration in the very languages – English, French and Portuguese – that Ngũgĩ would reject. In practice, however, such an argument ignores the achievement of African writers who have used the European languages to provide that alternative vision. In other words, English is one of the languages of Africa, at least for the present, because the poets have determined it so, a fact which is readily acknowledged by the African dictators who would silence them.

As I write, Jack Mapanje, the Malawian poet, has been in detention without charge or trial since September, 1987. According to rumour, our most reliable source of information, he is supposed to have said something to someone over a beer in the university bar. Be that as it may, the Ministry of Education and Culture has since declared his only collection to date, *Of Chameleons and Gods*, 'unsuitable for schools and colleges' because it expresses 'bitterness against the system'. This is the same system, incidentally, which banned Samuel Beckett's *Waiting for Godot* because the censor was distressed by 'the man with the rope around his neck', and which also banned the plays of Wole Soyinka, Africa's most distinguished writer, on the grounds that he was 'a bad man'. Beckett may or may not have said rude things about Malawi, but Soyinka was known to have called President-for-Life Dr Hastings Banda 'neurotic', an accurate enough description hardly calculated to endear him to the regime.

In terms of the continent's dictatorships, Malawi is only an extreme manifestation of the collective experience since independence in the early 1960's. It is virtually impossible to function as a writer in Africa without at some stage falling foul of the authorities. Among those represented in this anthology, Dennis Brutus, Wole Soyinka, Kofi Awoonor, Arthur Nortje and Frank Chipasula all suffered imprisonment or exile or both as a direct result of their work. Brutus and Chipasula continue to live in exile in the United States; Nortje committed suicide in a room in Oxford in 1970. He was 28 years old, five years younger than Christopher Okigbo, the celebrated Nigerian poet, who was killed by a stray bullet in the opening months of the civil war.

Imprisonment, exile, even death: the price that the poet might have to pay for giving voice to that collective experience accounts for the level of commitment which is the dominant feature of this anthology. So, for instance, Kojo Laing satirises 'the committees that march on the problems of the country' ('The same corpse'), Odia Ofeimun dedicates a poem 'to five journalists who cared' ('Beyond Fear'), and Frank Chipasula promises to 'undress our raped land and expose her wounds' ('Manifesto on *Ars Poetica*'). Even more forthright is Chipasula's 'First Word' to his long poem, '*NIGHTWATCHER: Nightsong*':

> This poem broke off the taproot of 'A Love Poem for My Country', which I wrote in February 1976 in response to the detention of eighteen young Malawian doctors lecturing at the University of Malawi. I had almost choked on a silence that is familiar to our people. It was a difficult poem to write in many ways, yet I had to break out of that vicious shell of silence . . .

This isn't to suggest that African writing is distinguished merely by its 'relevance', in itself a vulgar attitude, but that the need to respond to the conditions in the society is allied to the craft of poetry. Niyi Osundare, in the preface to his prize-winning collection, *The Eye of the Earth*, sees the poet as a 'visionary artist' for whom poetry is 'one of the weapons against a looming monster'. The obvious danger with such a view is that it easily degenerates into the kind of political sloganeering which passes for much of South African poetry; at its most creative, however, it forces the poet to stretch the resources of the language in order to properly confront the 'looming monster' that is squeezing the life-blood from the continent. This anthology attempts to include all those who have met this challenge.

ADEWALE MAJA-PEARCE, 1990

Mistakes are inevitable in an anthology of this kind. Profound apologies to Molara Ogundipe-Leslie and Syl Cheney-Coker, whose dates of birth are, respectively, 1940 and 1945.

ADEWALE MAJA-PEARCE, 1991

Dennis Brutus

Their Behaviour

Their guilt
is not so very different from ours:
– who has not joyed in the arbitrary exercise of
    power
or grasped for himself what might have been
    another's
and who has not used superior force in the
    moment when he could,
(and who of us has not been tempted to these
    things?) –
so, in their guilt,
the bared ferocity of teeth,
chest-thumping challenge and defiance,
the deafening clamour of their prayers
to a deity made in the image of their prejudice
which drowns the voice of conscience,
is mirrored our predicament
but on a social, massive, organised scale
which magnifies enormously
as the private deshabille of love
becomes obscene in orgies.

(*Blood River Day 1965*)

Postscripts 2

There are of course tho' we don't see them
– I cut away the public trappings to assert
certain private essentialities –
some heroic aspects of this all
– people outside admire, others pity –
but it is not of these I wish to speak;

but to pin down the raw experience
tease the nerve of feeling and expose
it in the general tissue we dissect;
and then, below this, with attentive ear
to hear the faint hearthrob –
a flicker, pulse, mere vital hint
which speaks of the stubborn will
the grim assertion of some sense of worth
in the teeth of the wind
on a stony beach, or among rocks
where the brute hammers fall unceasingly
on the mind.

A simple lust is all my woe:
the thin thread of agony
that runs through the reins
after the flesh is overspent
in over-taxing acts of love:

only I speak the others' woe:
those congealed in concrete
or rotting in rusted ghetto-shacks;
only I speak their wordless woe,
their unarticulated simple lust.

(*December 1971*)

Sometimes a mesh of ideas
webs the entranced mind,
the assenting delighted mental eye;
and sometimes the thrust and clash
of forged and metalled words
makes musical clangour in the brain;
and sometimes a nude and simple word
standing unlit or unadorned
may plead mutely in cold or dark
for an answering warmth, an enlightening
    sympathy;
state the bare fact and let it sing.

Nightsong: City

Sleep well, my love, sleep well:
the harbour lights glaze over restless docks,
police cars cockroach through the tunnel streets;

from the shanties creaking iron-sheets
violence like a bug-infested rag is tossed
and fear is immanent as sound in the wind-swung
    bell;

the long day's anger pants from sand and rocks;
but for this breathing night at least,
my land, my love, sleep well.

The sounds begin again;
the siren in the night
the thunder at the door
the shriek of nerves in pain.

Then the keening crescendo
of faces split by pain
the wordless, endless wail
only the unfree know.

Importunate as rain
the wraiths exhale their woe
over the sirens, knuckles, boots;
my sounds begin again.

Robben Island Sequence

I

neonbright orange
vermilion
on the chopped broken slate
that gravelled the path and yard
bright orange was the red blood
freshly spilt where the prisoners had passed;

and bright red
pinkbright red and light
the blood on the light sand by the sea
in pale lightyellow seas and
in the light bright airy air
lightwoven, seawoven, spraywoven air
of sunlight by the beach where we worked:

where the bright blade-edges of the rocks
jutted like chisels from the squatting rocks
the keen fine edges whitening to thinness
from the lightbrown masses of the sunlit rocks,
washed around by swirls on rushing wave water,
lightgreen or colourless, transparent with a hint of light:

on the sharp pale whitening edges
our blood showed light and pink,
our gashed soles winced from the fine barely felt slashes,
that lacerated afterwards:
the bloody flow
thinned to thin pink strings dangling
as we hobbled through the wet clinging sands
or we discovered surprised
in some quiet backwater pool
the thick flow of blood uncoiling
from a skein to thick dark red strands.

The menace of that bright day was clear as the blade of a
        knife;
from the blade edges of the rocks,
from the piercing brilliance of the day,
the incisive thrust of the clear air into the lungs
the salt-stinging brightness of sky and light on the eyes:
from the clear image, bronze-sharp lines of Kleynhans laughing
khaki-ed, uniformed, with his foot on the neck of the convict who
        had fallen,
holding his head under water in the pool where he had fallen
while the man thrashed helplessly
and the bubbles gurgled
and the air glinted dully on lethal gunbutts,
the day was brilliant with the threat of death.

II

sitting on the damp sand
in sand-powdered windpuff,
the treetops still grey in the early morning air
and dew still hanging tree-high,
to come to the beginning of the day
and small barely-conscious illicit greetings
to settle to a shape of mind, of thought,
and inhabit a body to its extremities:
to be a prisoner, a political victim,
to be a some-time fighter, to endure –
find reserves of good cheer, of composure
while the wind rippled the tight skin forming on the
                                        cooling porridge
and sandspray dropped by windgusts depressed it:
to begin, at the beginning of a day, to be a person
and take and hold a shape to last for this one day . . .

(afterwards the old lags came along
with their favourite warders, to select .
the young prisoners who had caught their eye,
so that these could be assigned to their span)

III

some mornings we lined up for 'hospital'
– it meant mostly getting castor oil –
but what a varied bunch we were!
for all had injuries – but in such variety
split heads; smashed ankles, arms;
cut feet in bandages, or torn and bloodied legs:
some, under uniform, wore their mass of bruises
but what a bruised and broken motley lot we were!

For My Sons & Daughters

Memory of me will be a process
of conscious and unconscious exorcism;
not to condemn me, you will need
forgetfulness of all my derelictions,
and kindness will be only yours
if you insist on clinging steadfastly
to some few small exaggerated symbols –
'This much he cared,' or 'Thus he did'
and 'If he could, he would have done much more.'

This I can understand, for my affection
enables me to penetrate the decades and your minds
and now I seek no mitigation –
would even welcome some few words of scorn;
but it might help if, reading this,
in after adult bitter years,
you are enabled then to say: 'He really cared then?'
'Really cared?' 'Our fictions have some substance then!'

I will not ask you then to add what I do now:
my loneliness; my failures; my amalgam wish to serve:
my continental sense of sorrow drove me to work
and at times I hoped to shape your better world.

Marjorie Oludhe Macgoye

Omera

In memory of Okot p'Bitek

So they have got you down at last, omera,
unmanned, incombatant, silenced, constrained,
bound in the noisy dark where small things burrow
and leaves that once waved high and proudly moulder.

So you will taste – what a one you were for tasting –
the soggy gobs of soil, the brittle fibres,
of roots from which earth crumbles in dry seasons,
the borers droning through the drowning silence.

So you are stilled – the long arm, sideways smile,
the arch, back-handed question, the arrogant
unhesitating machismo, all-embracing,
the eyes in the back of your head, the story-telling,

the tumbling lines, assertions, contradictions,
deep reverence underlying lightest words,
the fundamental kindness. You cannot live
by half-light or half-speaking or half-knowing.

So may the night be fierce for you with stars
blazing, with prowlers beautified in power,
dark traceries rounding into limbs and branches,
old stories lightened into touch and action.

Where homesteads crumbled, let again the pumpkin
take root and bind the soil, speaking beasts, singers
and sinuous dancers share all secrets with you –
tell how we, in the shadowy city, loved you.

August the First:
The Watchman Speaks

A life's spent guarding. What there is to guard
is not the question. On that day I found
myself off-guard, unmastered, not so much
free as free-swinging, out of compass, lost,
all I had seen ahead caught in the flood
of precious wasted oil and dirty blood.

A truncheon and a helmet to protect
my person and the woodyard. Limpid pop
of guns that caused no crying found me pacing
around the fence marking my master's bounds.
I did not know the measure of turmoil
to come, the wasted blood and dirty oil.

One of my boys was in the force, some neighbours
spotted him throwing clothes off as he ran.
In camp they kept them naked till the trial –
I see him shivering those twelve years ahead,
the sweat caked to his body, streaked with mud,
weighed down with wasted oil and dirty blood.

When the crowd came, what could a truncheon do
or claim of faithful service? I stood back
while they bent down the fence and scaled the yard
bare as a rocky hilltop, drove the lorry
into a lamp-post, blinded by the toil,
lumbering through wasted blood and dirty oil.

The path to distant home is heavy-hearted.
One child imprisoned, one who's learned to steal
and covets what's for stealing. Wife who wonders
why I have brought no dresses, why the job
is like to founder. What can be the good
of guarding wasted oil and dirty blood?

One aims to study, yet, they say, to read
is pestilential, perilous. I thought
knowledge of law would help us, but it seems
even law has its dangers. Let him choose
if he can use his knowledge as a foil
to beat off wasted blood and dirty oil.

The preacher says you tell the simple truth.
How can that be? I always have been taught
to tell what pleases, shows respect, conforms
to clan opinion and advantage. So
I did not see what happened to the wood,
dazzled by rainbow oil and flaming blood.

Does not each person play his role, to keep
order and office? If one laid heart bare,
wept with a woman's pang, grumbled at wage loss,
believed a stranger's promise, withheld a vote
from drunken kin, would not the world recoil
from private judgement, lacking blood and oil?

No, we accept our places, thus we dare not
expose the big cheat and so risk the small,
lose on our share of draws and empty acres,
the mother's brother's son's shaky diploma,
place in the cousin's treatment queue. What good
looking for better than the ties of blood?

Down in the valley fire spreads after fire,
leaping and licking greasy fingers after
the bone-dry tinders of the poor. To hide
in this inferno is near hell enough.
The rich once looted in their turn despoil
the bloodless hovels where folk queue for oil.

I have sat here day and night, bowing my head,
raised hands as ordered, guarded when I could
and not been thanked, given back what fell to me
and not been thanked for that. I only see
shambles, detritus, ragged clothing, mud,
pools of residual oil and dirty blood.

We sought for certain easements, but remained
bloated with old discomforts. Instruments
to cleanse us should be sharp and clean and wielded
with knowledge. Out of all our punctured hopes
remained the insipid matter from the boil,
voided in wasted blood and dirty oil.

What did they look for, those tall loose-limbed boys?
If for a kingdom and then turned aside
for bank-notes, gadgets, girls, they were not worthy
even to dream of kingdoms. Dream go rotten.
They had mislaid a purpose, soiled a good
in dirty pools of oil and wasted blood.

'They shall not grow old as we that are left grow old.'
Nor grow wise neither. There is cause to weep.
They 'should have died hereafter'. Distant voices
that made them drunk with words have no compassion
when joined in sentence, speak a strength to spoil,
spilled amid dirty blood and wasted oil.

Did they seek power or excitement, just
a fantasy of bloodshed? In old days
you could march outwards from a funeral
and cause more deaths to celebrate a death.
Did they expect to conquer death, who stood
defiled with wasted oil and dirty blood?

Or did they look for life along the way?
Think that we could afford the medicines
of health after such losses? Not remember
that time had taken what again must grow
before we reap, with painful sweat and toil,
replacement for the wasted blood and oil?

Some of them felt immune from death, as though
they drank the magic water; did they think,
young, able-bodied, shouting, they could pass
for neutral when the crunch came? Silent they lay
brain-spattered in the violence of a flood
retreating from rejected oil and blood.

Who then will guard us? Who observe the worn
jackets and shoes discarded when the new
seemed free for taking? They are wanted back
from drains and dustbins now. The missing persons
are wanted back. The dreams dragged through the mud
are wanted back with the spilt oil and blood.

Now there is dearth of noise, can there not be
a modest peace of plenty? May we read
if not deep books then deep designs for keeping
order and daylight decent and light-hearted?
The hum of workshops and shared warmth of soil
pulsing with healthy blood and useful oil?

I give my life to guarding, guarding the home
from want and violence, people that I love
from misuse and illusion, self from waste
and dirt and empty words. Guarding the land
to give in plenty of its needful good,
light from its oil and reverence for its blood.

August the First:
The Shadow. Patel Speaks

My granny used to say that if a shadow
of the unclean fell on you, then a curse
would follow. We all laughed, but now it seems
the shadow is upon us.

We left her there in India, brown, wrinkled,
peacefully glad a lifetime of neglect
had sheltered her from any palpable ill.
Her fading was unshadowed.

We condescended, confident in our schooling
and masculinity, returned to Kenya
southward and lofty-skied, where dawn and dark
cast a brief, slanting shadow.

True, we protected one another, did not
loose mother unescorted to the sun
of blazing noonday or the evening cool
when groups enjoy the shadow.

But in that small-town life, learning a language
    as pliant as our own, shuttering off
temple and school-house, thoughts and doubts and
    fears,
we did not heed the shadow.

There came a day of fear. We had not bargained
(in all our bargaining) to stand and measure
the size of our estrangement; handshakes, subscriptions
did not avert the shadow.

The girls, of course, are safe: the door was bolted
firmly upon them. Cloth and cash machines,
gold braid and bangles met desire enough
and overshadowed other lusts.

But when we meet to set the dowry forth
and give their innocence our best, come questions.
Boxed in from choice and daylight, yet their future
has been invaded by a shadow.

The pyres of those whose refuge was in burning
flame on our indecision: have we met
the gods' will truly if our caste still throws
a longer shadow than their virtue?

Goodwill and good intentions have not mastered
the separate demon or sequestered blessing.
We must invoke a more than natural light
to cast away the shadow.

August the First:
Court Martial. The Mother Speaks

I know – and yet I cannot share, as once
bruises and tears were kissed away.
I know – and yet I cannot share – compulsions
of mess and age-group strange to us older ones
who breathed conformity. I know
an ache that is like the second-born's after-pains,
an emptiness like your first going to school,
and awkwardness like your brief, cheerful notice
that you would marry soon. A cleaving together
like the first birth of grandchild.

I know the brittle porridge, the dried beans,
the greasy mugs with scum of tea on them.
I always kept your special cup and served you
the hottest meal from bottom of the pot.
The floors are grimy and they say cockroaches
crawl over them. I know the walls are slimy
with sweat and overcrowding and neglect.
The smell of misery vomited, yellow excrement
of bile nursed and insults swallowed
curdles from one to one, till the whole crew
of men holds its full breath, then sighs it out
with jokes and curses.

It is the same for all of you
whose hearts even your mothers do not know.
There is not one that has not grown
from bodies cherished, inched forth from a womb
with blood and silence. Every mother
knows smell of flesh, piss-pots, forced nakedness
and the unprecedented. Every birth
new eyes squinting in pain at a new world.

I know – you won't believe me – the questioning,
whether with lashes or potions it's the same,
or instruments searching where it hurts you most.
When did you, how did, why did, what reaction?
When the brain burns, and all you know to answer
is something comes to birth. Whether you planned
or counted costs or misread days or bled
or hungered is no matter. Done is done.

But though it is the same for all of you,
there is a special knowledge here within me
that slashes flesh from bone, thrusting through empty
womb into empty air, gasping for breath,
cold, sweaty, slimy, sharing
a birth-pang with my son.

Mathenge

Are you looking for me?

Why should you look for me if you have found
all you set out for? You agreed the terms.
I listened to those sent to talk us in
but faded away, distrusting Kinyanjui.
Are you looking for me?

In your Uhuru time there were some staying
still in the forest, homely. Like you they know
where honey curdles sweetly in the hive,
where the trap springs for meat, where water runs,
where leaves are dry and snug.

The foreign fish are bred there for the taking.
The screaming hyrax makes a warm soft garment.
If I decided so to stay, why hunt me
like the revengeful buffalo? In hiding
I do not harm you.

I once advanced with bugles at Othaya,
loud, like the ndete bird. The group of Forty
remember me, the oath of Olenguruone
went on resounding. That was a time of speaking.
Now is for silence.

Despite the ditch, the wire, the sharpened stakes,
the guards, the boards, the road-blocks and the passes,
the No-man's land where maize may not be grown,
did I not come among you in Shauri Moyo,
lend my voice to the Council?

You have entered the age of loud voices.
You need to eat at all hours, kindle your fires
incautiously, forget the rule of sharing.
Your fuel is brought in noisily. All must know
that you are cooking something.

If you are free your way, am I not free?
I see your antics as from the look-out post
we used to see the ditch and colony beyond.
I have earned the right to choice and there may be
some love from those I led.

You need the neon light, the photo flash.
Have you forgotten the dim, green forest light,
close limited, oblique, reflected so
that all our little vision must be sharp,
intelligent, directed?

You will not find me easily.

You, you have grown too careless to walk softly,
you pray too often at the same mugumo tree,
then they watch out for you, you blunder
like elephants through the forest, setting off
cracks of bamboo like rifles.

Your sentries fall asleep in the high branches,
the menace from the air unheralded
by warning cries, 'Kau, kau'. The monkeys taking refuge,
chattering at your side, are the first warning
of danger, and too late.

You have no earth at hand to damp your fires
at first alarm, then where's the earth you need
in the left hand for the ritual evening prayer?
Are simis sharp? There is more wit to praying
than empty-handed *thai* and *thai*.

You, you have lost your skill, with all your wealth
you're not provisioned to lie low. The urge
to move has blurred your subtlety, you pluck
the topmost buds that show, you spill the dew
cupped in the waiting leaf.

Look for me in the silence.

I creep among you, putting to shame your conceit.
You, whose attention is turned away to the sky-shout
you do not see the chameleon mocking your fear.
If you still seek me, turn your hearts to the silence,
alert to the forest.

The colobus has growled his evening call,
the blundering on the high boughs is stilled,
when the beasts have drunk their fill and are satisfied
only the bamboo groans and creaks to taunt you:
twittering has put birds to rest.

Look for me where the leaves have fallen thick
and the mush reshapes itself after the footfall,
where water runs softly, freeing the ear for caution,
or walking warily where bamboo rots underfoot
and fungus gleams in the dark.

The game trails are too risky for you now,
smelling of soap, not sweat, you don't look up
for high stalks smeared with mud from elephant ears.
You need landrovers, forcing a way into
the clearing, like foreign soldiers.

You of the rank and file, you still indulge
yourselves with women. Order is lost. Taboo
is violated. You no longer plait your hair
because you've no more fear of vermin, lose
the need to cleanse yourselves.

Your foreign tailors now equip you lightly.
Monkeys and bushbuck need no longer fear
your eager hunting. Fungus of bamboo
no longer cures your ills, or moss direct you,
crumbled into the wind.

Certainly there was blood,

blood and to spare. I've not forgotten either.
Blood of beast, interloper, enemy,
our own backsliders. Blood and excrement
of fear, and the unquestioned, awesome potion
that bound us more than will.

I do not forget, I who spoke soft and tried
to win wills willingly. You have become
too dainty for raw meat and raw enforcement
of what you hope to thrive on. Did you strangle
the careless only to avoid the blood?

I thought the time of killing past, but now
you squeeze to slow, pale endings by eviction,
delay in payments, hoarding, denigration,
leaving them whining, powerless to move,
like those old cattle, hamstrung.

Call me a butcher, slaughtering to live,
a furrier, an over-zealous guard,
a pest-controller or a simple soldier.
But do not call me leopard, killing by lust
only to feed the jackals.

On the high heath

look for me past the tree-line, scorched by heat
unshadowed in the day or frost at night.
Here there is open vision, the horizon
no longer hemmed by branches. Was this Kenya
that which I fought for?

Or in a foreign village seek me out
with a new wife and children who laugh to hear
the name of 'General'. I'm a kind of prophet
to those who fear my tales of winning freedom
but not believe them.

Do I look old to you? These are the old ones
clutching their fields and buses. Was there a wound?
Better be so than coughs and rheumatism
and despair, eating up those who fought with me
and never rate a pension.

Perhaps I crawled from the forest to the ditch
under a pile of charcoal sacks, and so
away, setting the dark and shaded forest,
crawling with life, helpful and hurtful, against
the antiseptic empty desert.

In deserts I have seen the only life
is what you put there. In your new republic
also the only life is what you put there.
I have fought enough for freedom, too tired to fight
for shambas and matatus.

Are you still looking for me? Ask of King'ori.
Below ground or above, Mathenge is watching
the harvest of his battle. Not to be taken
by ignorance, deceit or less than equal force,
that is the order of the day.

Where the neighbour's landmark has been moved,
Mathenge observes in silence. Where the franchise
passes from hand to hand, the son of Mirugi knows it.
Where the komereras come into their own,
still the lookout watches.

Facing the mountain, let your two hands be ready,
let there be intention of peace, let water be spilled
on the ground. Let taboos be respected,
thumbs grasped in recognition. No need to whisper
where is Mathenge?

*Note: Mathenge is the only 'Mau Mau general' not accounted for at the end of the forest fighting.

Christopher Okigbo

Thunder can Break

FANFARE of drums, wooden bells: iron chapter;
And our dividing airs are gathered home.

This day belongs to a miracle of thunder;
Iron has carried the forum
With token gestures. Thunder has spoken,
Left no signatures: broken

Barbicans alone tell one tale the winds scatter.

Mountain or tower in sight, lo, your hostages –
Iron has made, alas, masterpieces –
Statuettes of legendary heroes – iron birds
Held – fruit of flight – tight;

For barricaded in iron handiwork a miracle caged.

Bring them out we say, bring them out
Faces and hands and feet,
The stories behind the myth, the plot
Which the ritual enacts.

Thunder can break – Earth, bind me fast –
Obduracy, the disease of elephants.

Come Thunder

NOW THAT the triumphant march has entered the last street
 corners,
Remember, O dancers, the thunder among the clouds . . .

Now that laughter, broken in two, hangs tremulous between
 the teeth,
Remember, O dancers, the lightning beyond the earth . . .

The smell of blood already floats in the lavender-mist of the
 afternoon.
The death sentence lies in ambush along the corridors of
 power;
And a great fearful thing already tugs at the cables of the open
 air,
A nebula immense and immeasurable, a night of deep waters —
An iron dream unnamed and unprintable, a path of stone.

The drowsy heads of the pods in barren farmlands witness it,
The homesteads abandoned in this century's brush fire witness
 it:
The myriad eyes of deserted corn cobs in burning barns witness
 it:

Magic birds with the miracle of lightning flash on their
 feathers . . .

The arrows of God tremble at the gates of light,
The drums of curfew pander to a dance of death;

And the secret thing in its heaving
Threatens with iron mask
The last lighted torch of the century . . .

Hurrah for Thunder

WHATEVER happened to the elephant —
Hurrah for thunder —

The elephant, tetrarch of the jungle:
With a wave of the hand
He could pull four trees to the ground;
His four mortar legs pounded the earth:
Wherever they treaded,
The grass was forbidden to be there.

Alas! the elephant has fallen —
Hurrah for thunder —

But already the hunters are talking about pumpkins:
If they share the meat let them remember thunder.

The eye that looks down will surely see the nose;
The finger that fits should be used to pick the nose.

Today — for tomorrow, today becomes yesterday:
How many million promises can ever fill a basket . . .

If I don't learn to shut my mouth I'll soon go to hell,
I, Okigbo, town-crier, together with my iron bell.

Elegy for Slit-Drum

With rattles accompaniment

CONDOLENCES . . . from our swollen lips laden with
    condolences:

The mythmaker accompanies us
The rattles are here with us

condolences from our split-tongue of the slit drum condolences

one tongue full of fire
one tongue full of stone –

condolences from the twin-lips of our drum parted in
    condolences:

the panther has delivered a hare
the hare is beginning to leap
the panther has delivered a hare
the panther is about to pounce –

condolences already in flight under the burden of this century:

parliament has gone on leave
the members are now on bail
parliament is now on sale
the voters are lying in wait –

condolences to caress the swollen eyelids of bleeding mourners.

the cabinet has gone to hell
the timbers are now on fire
the cabinet that sold itself
ministers are now in gaol –

condolences quivering before the iron throne of a new
   conqueror:

the mythmaker accompanies us (*the Egret had come and gone*)
Okigbo accompanies us the oracle enkindles us
the Hornbill is there again (*the Hornbill has had a bath*)
Okigbo accompanies us the rattles enlighten us –

condolences with the miracle of sunlight on our feathers:

The General is up . . . the General is up . . . commandments . . .
the General is up the General is up the General is up –

condolences from our twin-beaks and feathers of condolences:

the General is near the throne
an iron mask covers his face
the General has carried the day
the mortars are far away –

condolences to appease the fever of a wake among tumbled
   tombs

the elephant has fallen
the mortars have won the day
the elephant has fallen
does he deserve his fate
the elephant has fallen
can we remember the date –

Jungle tanks blast Britain's last stand –

the elephant ravages the jungle
the jungle is peopled with snakes
the snake says to the squirrel
I will swallow you
the mongoose says to the snake
I will mangle you
the elephant says to the mongoose
I will strangle you

thunder fells the trees cut a path
thunder smashes them all – condolences . . .

THUNDER that has struck the elephant
the same thunder should wear a plume – condolences

a roadmaker makes a road
the road becomes a throne
can we cane him for felling a tree – condolences . . .

THUNDER that has struck the elephant
the same thunder can make a bruise – condolences:

we should forget the names
we should bury the date
the dead should bury the dead – condolences

from our bruised lips of the drum empty of condolences:

trunk of the iron tree we cry *condolences* when we break,
shells of the open sea we cry *condolences* when we shake . . .

Elegy for Alto

With drum accompaniment

AND THE HORN may now paw the air howling goodbye . . .

For the Eagles are now in sight:
Shadows in the horizon —

THE ROBBERS are here in black sudden steps of showers, of
    caterpillars —

THE EAGLES have come again,
The eagles rain down on us —

POLITICIANS are back in giant hidden steps of howitzers, of
    detonators —

THE EAGLES descend on us,
Bayonets and cannons —

THE ROBBERS descend on us to strip us of our laughter, of our
    thunder —

THE EAGLES have chosen their game,
Taken our concubines —

POLITICIANS are here in this iron dance of mortars, of
    generators —

THE EAGLES are suddenly there,
New stars of iron dawn;

So let the horn paw the air howling goodbye . . .

O mother mother Earth, unbind me; let this be
  my last testament; let this be
The ram's hidden wish to the sword the sword's
  secret prayer to the scabbard —

THE ROBBERS are back in black hidden steps of detonators —

FOR BEYOND the blare of sirened afternoons, beyond
  the motorcades;
Beyond the voices and days, the echoing highways; beyond
  the latescence
Of our dissonant airs; through our curtained eyeballs,
  through our shuttered sleep,
Onto our forgotten selves, onto our broken images;
  beyond the barricades
Commandments and edicts, beyond the iron tables,
  beyond the elephant's
Legendary patience, beyond his inviolable bronze
  bust; beyond our crumbling towers —

BEYOND the iron path careering along the same beaten track —

THE GLIMPSE of a dream lies smouldering in a cave,
  together with the mortally wounded birds.
Earth, unbind me; let me be the prodigal; let this be
  the ram's ultimate prayer to the tether . . .

AN OLD STAR departs, leaves us here on the shore
Gazing heavenward for a new star approaching;
The new star appears, foreshadows its going
Before a going and coming that goes on forever . . .

31

Lenrie Peters

Home Coming

The present reigned supreme
   Like the shallow floods over the gutters
Over the raw paths where we had been
   The house with the shutters

Too strange the sudden change
   Of the times we buried when we left
The times before we had properly arranged
   The memories that we kept

Our sapless roots have fed
   The wind-swept seedlings of another age
Cultivated weeds have grown where we led
   The virgins to the water's edge.

There at the edge of town
   Just by the burial ground
Stands the house without a shadow
   Lived in by new skeletons

That is all that is left
   To greet us on the home coming
After we have paced the world
   And longed for returning.

Isatou died
When she was only five
And full of pride
Just before she knew
How small a loss
It brought to such a few.
Her mother wept
Half grateful
To be so early bereft
And did not see the smile
As tender as the root
Of the emerging plant
Which sealed her eyes.
The neighbours wailed
As they were paid to do
And thought how big a spread
Might be her wedding too.
The father looked at her
Through marble eyes and said;
'Who spilt the perfume
Mixed with morning dew?'

I am asking about the way ahead,
the coarse road,
the Avenue autumnal with dust
erotic flashes of sunlight
snares in the forests' womb
the women pounding at evening
and the beating of breasts.

I am asking about times ahead,
the crude times,
times rancid and rough;
gunplay at the Bantaba
intimidations in the park,
heads floating down the river
human regatta in the dark.

I am asking about the price of rice
tomatoes, peppers, okras, spice
the four day week
half a meal a day
the unemployed and unemployable
with Ph.Ds for breakfast
and the sad sleek Mercedes in the closet.

Wole Soyinka

Fado Singer

for Amalia Roderiguez

My skin is pumiced to a fault
I am down to hair-roots, down to fibre filters
Of the raw tobacco nerve

Your net is spun of sitar strings
To hold the griefs of gods: I wander long
In tear vaults of the sublime

Queen of night torments, you strain
Sutures of song to bear imposition of the rites
Of living and of death. You

Pluck strange dirges from the storm
Sift rare stones from ashes of the moon, and rise
Night errands to the throne of anguish

Oh there is too much crush of petals
For perfume, too heavy tread of air on mothwing
For a cup of rainbow dust

Too much pain, oh midwife at the cry
Of severance, fingers at the cosmic cord, too vast
The pains of easters for a hint of the eternal.

I would be free of your tyranny, free
From sudden plunges of the flesh in earthquake
Beyond all subsidence of sense

I would be free from headlong rides
In rock seams and volcanic veins, drawn by dark steeds
On grey melodic reins.

Ogun Abibiman

March 3rd. 1976. Samora Machel. Leader of the People of Mozambique, announced to the world a symbolic decision which primed the black fuse on Southern Africa: the Mozambique nation had placed itself in a state of war against white-ruled Rhodesia.

But very few Africans see this as of primary relevance to the resolution of the Rhodesian anomaly, the act of Samora Machel being more profoundly self-evident as the definitive probe towards an ultimate goal, a summation of the continent's liberation struggle against the bastion of inhumanity – apartheid South Africa. It is best likened to the primary detonation of a people's collective will, the prelude to its absolute affirmation and manifestation. No longer do the natives of Abibiman ask of the void: 'Will it happen in my lifetime?' It *has* happened. The rest is history.

April 1976

From Ogun Abibiman I Induction

Steel Usurps the Forests;
Silence Dethrones Dialogue

No longer are the forests green. Storms
Assail the palm, the egret and the snail.
Bared, the dark heart of a hidden nursery
Of embers flares aglow, a landmass writhes
From end to end, bathed and steeped
In stern tonalities.

The boughs are broken, an earthquake
Rides upon the sway of chants, a flood
Unseasonal, a power of invocations.
Meander how it will, the river
Ends in lakes, in seas, in the ocean's
Savage waves. Our Flood's alluvial paths
Will spring the shrunken seeds;
Rains
Shall cleanse the leaves of blood.

A crop of arms dethrones the ancient
Reign of lush, compliant plains,
A truer fastness than the sanctuary of peace
In sermonising woods, and words, and wool
Over the vision of the ram – the knife
Caresses well, the victim bleats
A final testament of its contentment.

Tearless as dried leaves, whose stalks
Are sealed from waste, we shed green hopes
Of nature paths. Their trails are greener,
They, who violate the old preserves
With tracks of steel
And iron tracks, borne
Southward in His wake, to Veld and Cape
For the hour of our in-gathering.

A savage truth, the steel event
Shall even dislodge the sun if dark
Must be our aid. A savage memory raked
From veils of ashes, bores
Light tunnels through the years.
A horde of martyrs burst upon our present –
They march, beside the living.

Earth
Rings in unaccustomed accents
Time
Shudders at the enforced pace
Ogun
In vow of silence till the task is done,
Kindles the forge

*

Rust and silence fill the thatch
Of Ogun's farmstead. In corners of neglect –
Clods of dried earth, sweatrags, kernels,
A seed-yam's futile springing, a pithless coil
Sunlight seeking, guide ropes, stakes –
A planting season lost. Unswept, the woodflakes
Drift, the carver's craft abandoned. Mute,
A gesture frozen in ironwood, a shape arrested,
The adze on arc-point, motionless. Rust
Possesses cutlass and hoe. But listen . . .

Carillons in the distance. A festal
Anvil wreathed in peals, split by a fervid
Tongue of ore in whiteglow.
The Blacksmith's forearm lifts,
And dances . . .
Its swathes are not of peace.

Who dare restrain this novel form, this dread
Conversion of the slumbering ore, sealed
So long in patience, new stressed
To a keen emergence? – Witness –
Midwives of fireraze, heartburn, soulsear,
Of rooting out, of rack and mindscrew – witness –
Who dare intercede between
Hammer and anvil
In this fearsome weaning?

Huge with Time, a wombfruit lanced,
A Cycle resumed, the Craftsman's hand unclenches
To possess the hills and forests,
Pulses and habitations of men. Swayed
To chimes of re-creation, recalled
To an Origin, a oneness, witness
A burgeoning, a convergence of wills –
Nor god nor man can temper!

The singer's tongue is loosened
The drummer's armpits
Flex for a lyrical contention
For subterfuge has spent its course
And self-acclaiming,
Spurs the Cause to the season of enthronement.
Acolyte to Craftmaster of them all,
Medium of tremors from his taut membrane
I celebrate:

A cause that moves at last to resolution.
Prediction folds upon prediction till
The hour-glass is swallowed in its waspish
Waist, the sun engorged within
The black hole of the sky,
Time and space negated, epochs impacted
Flat, and all is in the present.

Gods shall speak to gods.
Stressed from the graveyards of our deities
Ogun goes to let ambrosia from profaning gods,
From skins of curd and sea-blue veins
To stir that claimed divinity of mind and limb
Whose prostrate planet is Abibimañ –
A black endowment since the cosmos spewed
Forth is tortured galaxies?

Let gods contend with gods.
All claims shall stand, till tested.
For we shall speak no more of rights
To the unborn bequeathed, nor will
To future hopes
The urgent mandates of our present.

Our vow of silence consecrates the act
For all, breaks the spell of feeble,
Cold resolve in Dialogue's illusion.
The sorcerers' wands are broken, weavers
Of consolation in the crystal glass
Of fractured sights.
Oh distanced statesmen, conciliators
Soon snared in slight cocoons of words!
Will you make a gift of gab to swollen tongues
Broken on the boot, and make their muteness
Proof of cravings for a Dialogue?

Sanctions followed Dialogue, games
Of time-pleading.
And Sharpeville followed Dialogue
And Dialogue
Chased its tail, a dogged dog
Dodging the febrile barks
Of Protest
Always from beyond the fence.
Sharpeville
Bared its teeth, and *that*
Proved no sleeping dog
Though the kind world let it lie.

Ogun is the tale that wags the dog
All dogs, and all have had their day.

For Dialogue
Dried up in the home of Protestations.
Sanctions
Fell to seductive ploys of Interests
Twin to dry-eyed arts of Expediency.
Diplomacy
Ran aground on Southern Reefs . . .

Pleas are ended in the Court of Rights. Hope
Has fled the Cape miscalled – Good Hope.

We speak no more of mind or grace denied
Armed in secret knowledge as of old.
In time of race, no beauty slights the duiker's
In time of strength, the elephant stands alone
In time of hunt, the lion's grace is holy
In time of flight, the egret mocks the envious
In time of strife, none vies with Him
Of seven paths, Ogun, who to right a wrong
Emptied reservoirs of blood in heaven
Yet raged with thirst – I read
His savage beauty on black brows.
In depths of molten bronze aflame
Beyond their eyes' fixated distances –
And tremble!

After the Deluge

Once, for a dare,
He filled his heart-shaped swimming pool
With bank notes, high denomination
And fed a pound of caviar to his dog.
The dog was sick; a chartered plane
Flew in replacement for the Persian rug.

He made a billion yen
Leap from Tokyo to Buenos Aires,
Turn somersaults through Brussels,
New York, Sofia and Johannesburg.
It cracked the bullion market open wide.
Governments fell, coalitions cracked
Insurrection raised its bloody flag
From north to south.

He knew his native land through iron gates,
His sight was radar bowls, his hearing
Electronic beams. For flesh and blood,
Kept company with a brace of Dobermans.
But – yes – the worthy causes never lacked
His widow's mite, discreetly publicized.

He escaped the lynch days. He survives.
I dreamt I saw him on a village
Water line, a parched land where
Water is a god
That doles its favors by the drop,
And waiting is a way of life.
Rebellion gleamed yet faintly in his eye
Traversing chrome-and-platinum retreats. There,
Hubs of commerce smoothly turn without
His bidding, and cities where he lately roosted
Have forgotten him, the preying bird
Of passage.

They let him live, but not from pity
Or human sufferance. He scratches life
From earth, no worse a mortal man than the rest.
Far, far away in dreamland splendor,
Creepers twine his gates of bronze relief.
The jade-lined pool is home
To snakes and lizards; they hunt and mate
On crusted algae.

Apologia (Nkomati*)

Doyen of walls,
Your puzzled frown has spanned the gulf
Between us.
Your stoic pride rejects, I fear,
This homage paid across four thousand miles,
Unfleshed at source, not manifested
In the act. Justice glowers in your rejection –
I submit:

Utterances flung like lead shot will never
Forge the chain mail of our collective will.
Only the salt of sweat-bathed palms
Pressed in anger will corrode
These prison bars. Our caged eagles
Wait on flight, their sweet-stern cry to stir
Our air again. Our assaulted patience
Waits in concert.

We wear our shame like bells on outcasts.
The snail has feet – I know; our jury
Shuffles to assemblage on the feet of snails.
These retreats in face of need
Betray our being – no wonder
The traitors steep us in contempt!

An old man of sixty-five ekes out his life
In prison slops. The poet
Strings you these lines, Mandela,
To stay from stringing lead.

---

*The Nkomati Accord: put simply, the nonagression pact between South Africa
and the front-line states.

'No!' He Said

For Nelson Mandela

Shorn of landmarks, glued to a sere promontory,
The breakers sought to crush his head,
To flush the black will of his race
Back in tidal waves, to flesh-trade centuries,
Bile-slick beyond beachcombing, beyond
Salvage operations but – no, he said.

Sea urchins stung his soul. Albino eels
Searched the cortex of his heart,
His hands thrust high to exorcise
Visions of lost years, slow parade of isolation's
Ghosts. Still they came, seducers of a moment's
Slack in thought, but – no, he said.

And they saw his hands were clenched.
Blood oozed from a thousand pores. A lonely
Fisher tensed against the oilcloth of new dawns,
Hand over hand he hauled. The harvest strained.
Cords turned writhing hawsers in his hands. 'Let go!'
The tempters cried, but – no, he said.

Count the passing ships. Whose argosies
Stretch like golden beads on far horizons? Those are
Their present ease, your vanished years. Castaway,
Minnows roost in the hold of that doomed ship
You launched in the eye of storms. Your mast is seaweed
On which pale plankton feed, but – no, he said.

Are you bigger than Nkomati? Blacker
Than hands that signed away a continent for ease?
Lone matador with broken paddle for a lance,
Are you the Horn? The Cape? Sequinned
Constellation of the Bull for tide-tossed
Castaways on pallid sands? No, he said.

The axis of the world has shifted. Even the polar star
Loses its fixity, nudged by man-made planets.
The universe has shrunk. History reechoes as
We plant new space flags of a master race.
You are the afterburn of our crudest launch.
The stars disown you, but – no, he said.

Your tongue is salt swollen, a mute keel
Upended on the seabed of forgotten time.
The present breeds new tasks, same taskmasters.
On that star planet of our galaxy, code-named Bantustan,
They sieve rare diamonds from moon dust. In choice reserves,
Venerably pastured, you . . . but – no, he said.

That ancient largesse on the mountaintop
Shrinks before our gift's munificence, an offer even
Christ, second-come, could not refuse. Be ebony mascot
On the flagship of our space fleet, still
Through every turbulence, spectator of our Brave New
    World.
Come, Ancient Mariner, but – no, he said –

No! I am no prisoner of this rock, this island,
No ash spew on Milky Ways to conquests old or new.
I am this rock, this island. I toiled,
Precedent on this soil, as in the great dark whale
Of time, Black Hole of the galaxy. Its maw
Turns steel-wrought epochs plankton – yes – and
Vomits our new worlds.

In and out of time warp, I am that rock
In the black hole of the sky.

Kofi Awoonor

Songs of Sorrow

Dzogbese Lisa has treated me thus
It has led me among the sharps of the forest
Returning is not possible
And going forward is a great difficulty
The affairs of this world are like the chameleon faeces
Into which I have stepped
When I clean it cannot go.*

I am on the world's extreme corner,
I am not sitting in the row with the eminent
But those who are lucky
Sit in the middle and forget
I am on the world's extreme corner
I can only go beyond and forget.

My people, I have been somewhere
If I turn here, the rain beats me
If I turn there the sun burns me
The firewood of this world
Is only for those who can take heart
That is why not all can gather it.
The world is not good for anybody
But you are so happy with your fate;
Alas! the travellers are back
All covered with debt.

*Colloquial: It (the faeces) will not go (come off).

Something has happened to me
The things so great that I cannot weep;
I have no sons to fire the gun when I die
And no daughters to wail when I close my mouth
I have wandered on the wilderness
The great wilderness men call life
The rain has beaten me,
And the sharp stumps cut as keen as knives
I shall go beyond and rest.
I have no kin and no brother,
Death has made war upon our house;

And Kpeti's great household is no more,
Only the broken fence stands;
And those who dared not look in his face
Have come out as men.
How well their pride is with them.
Let those gone before take note
They have treated their offspring badly.
What is the wailing for?
Somebody is dead. Agosu himself
Alas! a snake has bitten me
My right arm is broken,
And the tree on which I lean is fallen.

Agosu if you go tell them,
Tell Nyidevu, Kpeti, and Kove
That they have done us evil;
Tell them their house is falling
And the trees in the fence
Have been eaten by termites;
That the martels curse them.
Ask them why they idle there
While we suffer, and eat sand,
And the crow and the vulture
Hover always above our broken fences
And strangers walk over our portion.

The Weaver Bird

From three poems from Rediscovery *(1964)*

The weaver bird built in our house
And laid its eggs on our only tree
We did not want to send it away
We watched the building of the nest
And supervised the egg-laying.
And the weaver returned in the guise of the owner
Preaching salvation to us that owned the house
They say it came from the west
Where the storms at sea had felled the gulls
And the fishers dried their nets by lantern light
Its sermon is the divination of ourselves
And our new horizons limit at its nest
But we cannot join the prayers and answers of the
                                 communicants.
We look for new homes every day,
For new altars we strive to rebuild
The old shrines defiled by the weaver's excrement.

America

A name only once
crammed into the child's fitful memory
in malnourished villages,
vast deliriums like the galloping foothills of the Colorado:
of Mohawks and the Chippewa,
horsey penny-movies
brought cheap at the tail of the war
to Africa. Where indeed is the Mississippi panorama
and the girl that played the piano &
kept her hand on her heart
as Flanagan drank a quart of moonshine
before the eyes of the town's gentlemen?
What happened to your locomotive in Winter, Walt,
and my ride across the prairies in the trail
of the stage-coach, the gold-rush and the Swanee river?
Where did they bury Geronimo,
heroic chieftain, lonely horseman of this apocalypse
who led his tribesmen across deserts of cholla
and emerald hills
in pursuit of despoilers,
half-starved immigrants
from a despoiled Europe?
What happened to Archibald's
soul's harvest on his raw earth
of raw hates?
To those that have none
a festival is preparing at graves' ends
where the mockingbird's hymn
closes evening of prayers
and supplication as
new winds blow from graves
flowered in multi-colored cemetaries even
where they say the races are intact.

From Long Island Sketches

x: On having been an experimental sacred cow for four years, and a token African on Faculty.

It first began when sitting in the huge auditorium
in the gym, a member of the curious audience
who wants to hear the President answer black students
demands, I heard my name booming across the hall; the impact,
being so sudden, denied me any understanding of exactly in
connection with what my sacred name was called. But let it be.

Four years, teaching a motley group of students well
motivated, desirous of knowledge of Africa and vaguely
familiar with my little reputation as a teacher (in spite of
the teacher evaluation's strenuous effort to say I was stiff
and British, a double insult).

We vaulted through tribal woes
grim battles between clansmen and conquerors
jazzed up versions of historical struggles
reduced to neat novellas; we laughed
learned, sang, and exchanged greetings in
obscure African languages, died
upon our knees in this grim desert
My sympathies were with the youth,
with the dumbheads covered by overgrowths of hair
and lack of bath-water, tattered rich kids
from Jewish suburbia, alarmed at what the world is
and prostrate before a bemused singleminded fool.

From Songs of Abuse

ii: To the Eminent Scholar and Meddler

You showed your dirty face first in Detroit
slandered me, in your ugly missionary voice.
If the season were right
I would have broken your bones across my knees.
I heard you have taken to playing an accordian
in the Washington night scaring foreign diplomats
with your horror show.
You joined the revolutionaries of Azania
only to betray them for multi-colored blankets
and a battered copy of the Pilgrim's Progress.
You were caught eating hog in a synagogue in Rome,
uttering profanities during a rain dance in Navajo country,
screaming the sacred name of the Buddha across the Punjabi
                                                    plain
taking a shit in a shinto shrine in Kyoto.
What manner of man are you?
a despoiler of natives, traducer of tribes and clans,
abuser of ancient homesteads?
Remember the night you were drunk in a tavern in Algiers
and I had to bail you out with my last dollar
and you turned around and insulted my mother,
You know your morality is a cheap alibi
for your lack of scholarship, an apology for your bad verse.
When we meet at the court of Prempeh, I will recount
all the historical oaths you broke,
and push the lie down your black throat.

From Hymns of Praise, Celebration, and Prayer

ii: To Dennis Brutus

At first from your verse
the imprecise dilletante
a cocky troubadour, professional exile,
chronicler of sirens knuckles and boots
through Texan nights
and Louisiana plains, in jazz-halls
and strip-joints, beneath spinning buttocks'
    of dancing girls warm
beyond the stars' surmising, a warrior
without a country, a rain cloud
falling in alien lands, a rainbow
of arched serpents
a revolutionary in necktie,
friend of Shakespeare, Wordsworth
and the sirens of your Cape
that will sing you home on rainbows
    someday, I will reiterate your mortality
    when our bones and spirits will not crunch.

From Afro-American Beats

iii: An American Memory of Africa

Black as my night, anonymous here
my death in Elizabethville was your death.
Blood shed in Sharpeville was shed before in Ulundi
Alabama, Memphis
Fred Hampton on a Chicago bed
blood and gun fire in darkness
was it prophesied that the panther
shall die in his bed without a leap?
I hug my black skin here against my better judgement
hung my shields and sheaves for a season.
Leaving Africa that September 1967
in flight from the dreams we built
in the pale talons of eagles yard
donkeys braying on the bloody field across the square
the bulge of my sails unfurl for the
harbor of hate;
The pride of this color
by which they insist on defining my objection:
that I am a nigger is no matter
but that I died in Memphis and Elizabethville
outrages my self-esteem
I plot my vengeance silently
like Ellison's man in bright dens
of hiding and desperate anonimity
and with the hurricanes and eagles of tomorrow
prepare a firm and final rebuttal to your lies.
To be delivered in the season of infinite madness.

From The House by the Sea (1978)

The First Circle

1

the flat end of sorrow here
two crows fighting over New Year's Party
leftovers. From my cell, I see a cold
                hard world.

2

So this is the abscess that
        hurts the nation –
        jails, torture, blood
                and hunger.
One day it will burst;
        it must burst.

3

When I heard you were taken
we speculated, those of us at large
where you would be
in what nightmare will you star?
That night I heard the moans
wondering whose child could now
be lost in the cellars of oppression.
Then you emerged, tall, and bloody-eyed.
It was the first time
            I wept.

4

      The long nights I dread most
     the voices from behind the bars
   the early glow of dawn before
the guard's steps wake me up,
the desire to leap and stretch
and yawn in anticipation
of another dark home-coming day
only to find that
     I cannot.
     riding the car into town
hemmed in between them
     their guns poking me in the ribs,
     I never had known that my people
     wore such sad faces, so sad
     they were on New Year's Eve,
     so very sad.

J. P. Clark Bekederemo

Abiku

Coming and going these several seasons,
Do stay out on the baobab tree,
Follow where you please your kindred spirits
If indoors is not enough for you.
True, it leaks through the thatch
When floods brim the banks,
And the bats and the owls
Often tear in at night through the eaves,
And at harmattan, the bamboo walls
Are ready tinder for the fire
That dries the fresh fish up on the rack.
Still, it's been the healthy stock
To several fingers, to many more will be
Who reach to the sun.
No longer then bestride the threshold
But step in and stay
For good. We know the knife scars
Serrating down your back and front
Like the beak of the sword-fish,
And both your ears, notched
As a bondsman to this house,
Are all relics of your first comings.
Then step in, step in and stay,
For her body is tired,
Tired, her milk going sour
Where many more mouths gladden the heart.

The casualties

To Chinua Achebe

The casualties are not only those who are dead;
They are well out of it.
The casualties are not only those who are wounded,
Though they await burial by instalment.
The casualties are not only those who have lost
Persons or property, hard as it is
To grope for a touch that some
May not know is not there.
The casualties are not only those led away by night;
The cell is a cruel place, sometimes a haven,
Nowhere as absolute as the grave.
The casualties are not only those who started
A fire and now cannot put it out. Thousands
Are burning that had no say in the matter.
The casualties are not only those who escaping
The shattered shell become prisoners in
A fortress of falling walls.

The casualties are many, and a good number well
Outside the scenes of ravage and wreck;
They are the emissaries of rift,
So smug in smoke-rooms they haunt abroad,
They do not see the funeral piles
At home eating up the forests.
They are the wandering minstrels who, beating on
The drums of the human heart, draw the world
Into a dance with rites it does not know

The drums overwhelm the guns . . .
Caught in the clash of counter claims and charges
When not in the niche others have left,
We fall,
All casualties of the war,
Because we cannot hear each other speak,
Because eyes have ceased to see the face from the crowd,
Because whether we know or
Do not know the extent of wrong on all sides,
We are characters now other than before
The war began, the stay-at-home unsettled
By taxes and rumours, the looters for office
And wares, fearful every day the owners may return,
We are all casualties,
All sagging as are
The cases celebrated for kwashiorkor,
The unforeseen camp-follower of not just our war.

Epilogue to Casualties

To Michael Echeruo

In the East Central State of Nigeria, four years
After the war, I visited again the old sites
I had frequented with friends, dead
Or gone now to their own homesteads,
Admonished gently by the administrator
Of the estate for coming when reconstruction work
Was all but complete. Even then,
The ruins that greeted me on the road,
Right from Milliken Hill to the amputated
Giant astride the River Niger, raised

Before my eyes a vision of the unnatural
Disaster that is war: the bridges,
Broken before and beyond Oji,
The bellows belching again at Awka,
The skeleton carriers, camouflaged
By grass at Abagana, and of course,
The other Ogidi, strangely without
Pock-marks, hamlet of the fabulist
Who I thought would never forgive, never forget,
Knowing the wrong in his own heart.
Yet Onitsha, whether as the birthplace
Of Emmanuel Ifeajuna, Tony Asika,
Or Nnamdi Azikiwe, came as the jolt
That broke my journey to Owerri,
Aba, Umuahia, through Ulli
Ihiala which after all was but a stretch
Of road for pirate planes to spirit off
Warriors, swearing to fight to the last man
Even as they fled orphan, widow, and batman.
Here houses, scalped and scarred past surgery,
Stared at me, sightless in their sockets, like
The relics of shell-shock that they are.
One, so mutilated, it is a miracle
The parts hung together at all,
Called to me in the crush, in it one
Plump woman, careless of her bare breast
And brood, pounding yam up on a balcony,
Tilted in face of gravity. The wreck
Seemed greatest by the river, there
Voiceless and sweeping the earth as
A widow who has also buried her seeds.
To one side of her lay that giant bridge
With knee lopped in the air, while clamorous
For comfort upon her other side struggled
The old market of dreams, a forest,

Cropped of all foliage, rising already
Above two cathedral spires still in conflict
For eastern pastures, as they were before the war.

The News from Ethiopia and the Sudan

Armies and lemmings do not go
In numbers such as come over
In waves everyday from the Sudan
And Ethiopia. All down
The Saharan belt, land that once
    feasted
Pharaohs and emperors no longer
Can feed livestock and peasant,
Though out in commons, millions fled
Yesterday, milk and grain
Are building lakes and pyramids,
Protected well by thirteen tribes.
How have fields that first heard
The hurrah of harvest and hunt
Become the burning grounds for cattle
And sheep no powers, past
Or present, will take for offering?
Where has the flock wandered
That father and mother beggar
Scarecrows in the field, all their seeds
Wilting at their breasts and feet?
The prophets spoke of seasons
Of plagues and pestilence;
They spoke of visitations
Of frogs, rats, locusts and bats;
They also spoke of the ruler
Who acted upon a dream, and turned

Seven lean years into a festival
In fields where the wind also blew
Sand in the face of the sun.
In our times, so briefly touched
By the string of troubadours, the
    mighty
Of the earth hear and see all right,
But are for their arms and skin alone.

A Family Procession

It seems no day passes now
But yet another child is taken home
To be laid at the foot of one tree.
From all across the country they come
In one traffic as traders to a fair,
Except that each arrival empties
A house that swelled so like a market,
From the first tide, it was heard
On shores at the other side of the sea.
Who next in line in a line,
Stretched fourteen times round itself?
What commodities of another world,
Displayed only to its chosen ones,
And what accounts, left to settle
In the ruins of their numinous yard,
Bring them home to a market now
A burial-ground among the creeks
Of a great river no vessels plow?
As all the world on the road watches
And waits with wonder, a family,
Perhaps more than five thousand strong,
Trembles to announce its latest dead.

Death of a Lady

Death can be so lazy at times
On purpose he took many months
Claiming a lady nobody knew
Attracted him for years more than
Her sisters much riper in
All things a man wants. Although
She cried from time to time he had
His hand early on her breast,
None saw a lamb under the paw
Of a leopard, so filled with flesh
From the forest, it played
With a pet dish as a spoilt child
Does before his mother. And not
Until she had learnt to breathe
Again with everybody believing
The leopard had gone back
Into the bush did he turn
And take her piece by piece,
As a cob of corn is picked
Between thumbs, in the end
Her eyes that refused to close
In death threw a green suffused light
Upon the bare pole of her body,
Asking: 'Who now will he take?'

The Order of the Dead

The dead in other lands are settled
In communes away from town, and although
Town in time may grow to encircle commune,
The dead of other lands sleep sound
Within their walls, and no amount
Of traffic, screaming outside their gates,
Can wake them from their set dream
Of another land. But here in a land
Where the dead without blemish
Are buried in their homesteads, if blessed
With children, and in their own bedrooms,
Taken over by their heirs, if titles
Are clean, the dead do not sleep
Any more than a mother beside
Her troubled child at dead of night.
They are of an order coming after death,
Though going before birth to that source
Which is the home for all
That inhabit the land. Knowing no fixed day
That all the dead of the world must wake,
They are quick to rise, whenever there is
The slither of a snake in the house,
And all the town has no stick
Long enough to strike it dead.
And while long lines of descendants serve them,
The dead of this land, praising God,
May come again into town as children,
If at their first coming,
They went away with a sign of great wrong.

Syl Cheney-Coker

Letter to a Tormented Playwright

For Yulisa Amadu Maddy

Amadu I live alone inside four walls of books
some I have read others will grow cobwebs
or maybe like some old friends and lovers
will fade away with their undiscovered logic

the world that I have seen: New York
where I suffered the suicidal brother
and London where I discovered Hinostroza
Delgado, Ortega, Heraud and the other
Andean poets with a rage very much like ours!

remember Amadu how terrible I said it was
that you were in exile and working
in the Telephone Office in touch with all
the languages of the world but with no world
to call your own; how sad you looked that winter
drinking your life and reading poetry with me
in the damp chilly English coffee shops

*

remember I said how furious I was
that Vallejo had starved to death in Paris
that Rabearivelo had killed himself
suffocated by an imaginary France
and I introduced Neruda and Guillen to you
and how in desperation we sought solace in the house
of John La Rose, that courageous Trinidadian poet

Amadu I am writing to you from the dungeon of my heart
the night brings me my grief and I am passive
waiting for someone to come, a woman
a friend, someone to soothe my dying heart!
now the memory of our lives brings a knife to my poems
our deaths which so burdened the beautiful Martiniquan
you said made you happy, she made you so happy, you a
tormented playwright

*

sadness returns, the apparitions of my brothers
and my mother grows old thinking about them
and also seeing so much sadness in me her living and dying son
my mother who wishes me happy, who wants me to relive the
                                                        son
she lost to poetry like a husband a wife to a trusted friend

but already the walls are closing around me
the rain has stopped and once again I am alone
waiting for them, the politicians of our country to come for me
to silence my right to shouting poetry loud in the parks
but who can shut up the rage the melodrama of being Sierra
                                                        Leone
the farce of seeing their pictures daily in the papers
the knowledge of how though blindfolded and muzzled
something is growing, bloating, voluptuous and not despairing
I say to you for now, I embrace you brother.

On Being a Poet in Sierra Leone

A poet alone in my country
I am seeking the verisimilitudes in life
the fire of metaphors the venom of verse
my country you are my heart living like a devastated landscape
always the magic of being underground of burying truth
of shedding your metaphysical form
country I wish to die being your poet
I who have so condemned and sold you
I who have so loved and hated you
imagine my sadness, the poetry of being you
a colossus strangled by fratricidal parasites
have I betrayed you writing my hermetic poetry
I suffer the estrangement of being too 'intellectual'
at the university the professors talk about the poetry
of Syl Cheney-Coker condemning students
to read me in the English honours class
my country I do not want that!
do not want to be cloistered in books alone
I want to be the albatross learning and living your fits
I want only to plough your fields
to be the breakfast of the peasants who read
to help the fishermen bring in their catch
I want to be your national symbol of life
because my heart is heavy country and exile calls
beating the pangs of oblivion on my brow
I want once more like the common man
to love a woman without dying of love
to leave a son or daughter to remember my grave
country you my pain, my phoenix, my disastrous gloating
                                        python

in whose belly all my anger dies
I am going to be happy to stop carrying my pain

like a grenade in my heart, I want to be simple
if possible to live with you, and then one day die leaving
my poetry, an imperfect metaphor of life!

The Outsider

Armed with his crutches, the thief, wolf-like,
steals from the tree; crucify him for that,
or the woman forsaking her child to kiss
the angelic feet of Mary Magdalene; stone her for that

observe the cripples painted by Bruegel
skinning the corpse of a dog; call out
the sanitary van for that, or the crazed
desecrating the dowager's gown; cauterize him for that

draining his glass of resin the neophyte prays
before a God supine, he prays before a resonant stone
dicephalous existence, the godhead bad, the godhead good
thinking how they have released him but not his soul

alone, his soul comes seeking that which was stolen
from him, the pilgrim's path to faith, his soul
is a crown of thorns, the girl with the harelip
is his soul destroyed, that man at the foot of Golgotha
lonely beginning lonely redemption

lifting his chain O Lord, give him the text
of your annunciation! for who would dine released
from your cross when the pastoral is lost?

in the hour of your trial Lord
deliver from your cross your brother Barabbas!

Arthur Nortje

Letter from Pretoria Central Prison

The bell wakes me at 6 in the pale spring dawn
with the familiar rumble of the guts negotiating
murky corridors that smell of bodies. My eyes
find salutary the insurgent light of distances.
Waterdrops rain crystal cold, my wet
face in ascent from an iron basin
greets its rifled shadow in the doorway.

They walk us to the workshop. I am eminent,
the blacksmith of the block: these active hours
fly like sparks in the furnace, I hammer metals
with zest letting the sweating muscles
forge a forgetfulness of worlds more magnetic.
The heart, being at rest, life peaceable,
your words filter softly through my fibres.

Taken care of, in no way am I unhappy,
being changed to neutral. You must decide
today, tomorrow, bear responsibility,
take gaps in pavement crowds, refine ideas.
Our food we get on time. Most evenings
I read books, Jane Austen
for elegance, agreeableness (Persuasion).

Trees are green beyond the wall, leaves through the mesh
are cool in sunshine
among the monastic white flowers of spring that floats
prematurely across the exercise yard, a square
of the cleanest stone I have ever walked on.
Sentinels smoke in their boxes, the wisps
curling lovely through the barbed wire.

Also music and cinema, yesterday double feature.
At 4 pm it's back to the cell, don't laugh
to hear how accustomed one becomes. You spoke
of hospital treatment – I see the smart nurses
bringing you grapefruit and tea – good
luck to the troublesome kidney.
Sorry there's no more space. But date your reply.

(*August 1966*)

Newcombe at the Croydon Gallery

The dealer in shirt-sleeves told his assistant Jenny
to serve champagne to a tall supercilious lady.
Middle-aged Americans in sneakers,
peering closely, noses to the gouaches,
jostled the dainty natives, and a Rolling
Stone in executive grey arrived
without a murmur among the objets d'art.
Upstairs against the ebony panels
under the chromium lamps a woman stood
deciding to buy Bill Newcombe's watercolour.

A small posh opening in the arcade
with suave young professionals, he the self-taught
veteran shown in Paris,
Sydney, Moscow, San Francisco, New York,
props himself on his stiff leg, looking bland,
back now, still in exile, on an island.
Across the strait, with a view of Vancouver
he built sand castles, trapped birds in his boyhood,
cut timber before the war, started creating
those weird spindly shapes which sang
the lyric of the standing birch along the pulsing blood,
peeled lean and white.
                    The Royal Air Force
claimed for a space of time his gift.

Hence experience is learning:
no violent punctures, interrogation rooms,
surrealistic phalluses or soup tins inspire him.
There are no birds, guitars, or flowerpots.
His flimsy tumbling squares
seek each other at normal moments
where line and tint converge,
the anguish being level with the eye,
yet not concealing any of the gaiety.

Tonight the private view goes on too long:
he grumbles sceptically, blames his Welsh wife.
Nervy, she shakes her rosé,
offering me a cigarette.

From an iron pit close to the twinkling stars
he peeped tinily into a hell of flak,
the lights bouncing between long stretches of dark.
Or he tattooed the visible sky with smokeplumes
cooped in the bell of a steel dog
till shrapnel studded his ribs with scarlet jewels.
But it is twenty years later or so that I hear
the story in bits and pieces.
We are drinking Spanish sauternes
in the top flat of a brick house, Highgate, London,
and winter returns to the landing:
the owls hoot at night.

Now that I travel away I remember
the soft greys of autumn, the ambers of autumn,
the quickness of seasons, occasions that change,
the din that rises from the lobby where
a Pakistani in a dressing-gown
natters over the telephone,
and our wine-rich laughter while
over the cold fields the thick air settles.

In retrospect appears his face
complete with puckish wrinkles
underwritten by the grey goatee:
though I have also seen at dusk
thin leaf-blades of his eyes observe austerely
the feeble warmth that now is alone available.
To survive, may he have meant,
one must choose the possible.

(*Oxford, December 1966*)

Waiting

The isolation of exile is a gutted
warehouse at the back of pleasure streets:
the waterfront of limbo stretches panoramically –
night the beautifier lets the lights
dance across the wharf.
I peer through the skull's black windows
wondering what can credibly save me.
The poem trails across the ruined wall
a solitary snail, or phosphorescently
swims into vision like a fish
through a hole in the mind's foundation, acute
as a glittering nerve.

Origins trouble the voyager much, those roots
that have sipped the waters of another continent.
Africa is gigantic, one cannot begin
to know even the strange behaviour furthest
south in my xenophobic department.
Come back, come back mayibuye
cried the breakers of stone and cried the crowds
cried Mr. Kumalo before the withering fire
mayibuye Afrika

Now there is the loneliness of lost
beauties at Cabo de Esperancia, Table Mountain:
all the dead poets who sang of spring's
miraculous recrudescence in the sandscapes of Karoo
sang of thoughts that pierced like arrows, spoke
through the strangled throat of multi-humanity
bruised like a python in the maggot-fattening sun.

You with your face of pain, your touch of gaiety,
with eyes that could distil me any instant
have passed into some diary, some dead journal
now that the computer, the mechanical notion
obliterates sincerities.

The amplitude of sentiment has brought me no nearer
to anything affectionate,
new magnitude of thought has but betrayed
the lustre of your eyes.

You yourself have vacated the violent arena
for a northern life of semi-snow
under the Distant Early Warning System:
I suffer the radiation burns of silence.
It is not cosmic immensity of catastrophe
that terrifies me:
it is solitude that mutilates,
the night bulb that reveals ash on my sleeve.
(*1967*)

Autopsy

I

My teachers are dead men. I was too young
to grasp their anxieties, too nominal an exile
to mount such intensities of song;
knowing only the blond
colossus vomits its indigestible
black stepchildren like autotoxins.

Who can endure the succubus?
She who had taught them proudness of tongue
drank an aphrodisiac, then swallowed
a purgative to justify the wrong.
Her iron-fisted ogre of a son
straddled the drug-blurred townships,
breathing hygienic blasts of justice.

Rooted bacteria had their numbers
swiftly reduced in the harsh sunlight of arc-lamps,
the arid atmosphere where jackboots scrape
like crackling electric, and tape recorders
ingest forced words like white corpuscles,
until the sterile quarantine of dungeons
enveloped them with piteous oblivion.

In the towns I've acquired
arrive the broken guerillas, gaunt and cautious,
exit visas in their rifled pockets
and no more making like Marx
for the British Museum in the nineteenth century,
damned: the dark princes, burnt and offered
to the four winds, to the salt-eyed seas. To their earth
unreturnable,
           The world receives
them, Canada, England now that the laager
masters recline in a gold inertia
behind the arsenal of Sten guns. I
remember many, but especial one
almost poetic, so undeterrable.

II

He comes from knife-slashed landscapes:
I see him pounding in his youth across red sandfields
raising puffs of dust at his heels,
outclassing the geography of dongas
mapped by the ravenous thundery summers.
He glided down escarpments like the wind, until
pursued by banshee sirens
he made their wails the kernel of his eloquence,
turning for a time to irrigate
the stretches of our virgin minds.

Thus – sensitive precise
he stood with folded arms in a classroom
surveying a sea of galvanized roofs,
transfixed as a chessman, only
with deep inside his lyric brooding,
the flame-soft bitterness of love that recrudesces;
O fatal loveliness of the land
seduced the laager masters to disown us.

36,000 feet above the Atlantic
I heard an account of how they had shot
a running man in the stomach. But what isn't told
is how a warder kicked the stitches open
on a little-known island prison which used to be
a guano rock in a sea of diamond blue.

Over the phone in a London suburb he sounds
grave and patient – the years have stilled him:
the voice in a dawn of ash, moon-steady,
is wary of sunshine which has always been
more diagnostic than remedial.

The early sharpness passed beyond to noon
that melted brightly into shards of dusk.
The luminous tongue in the black world
has infinite possibilities no longer.

Asseverations

The fire will not ask me to make its bed,
nor is there more than one room in the womb:
cold stone stands above you or instead
your ashes have been scattered in the wind.

Drops of compassion in the oceans of
humanity are bitterly invisible:
the rice-field and the rose-garden must blend
before the hand that sowed can waft in harvest.

Words I plant in this cool adversity
germinate in April ardour, green
fused push through sleep mist that has haunted
the rich black soil of midnight in the brain,

I ghost-wrote tales in Africa, pseudonymous and,
hunched in shack or hovel in pursuit
of truths in rhythms, nocturnes, melodies:
grappled with the hardship of a rhyme.

The liberators are unnameable,
with winter in their hair perhaps, themselves
hexed, or fall in the rape of grass,
whose recipes are now illegible.

Out of such haze, such loss, the luck of birth,
must be fashioned never questionably
strength of seed and courage of decision.
There is never work without resistance.

Native's Letter

Habitable planets are unknown or too
far away from us to be
of consequence. To be of
value to his homeland must the wanderer

not weep by northern waters, but love
his own bitter clay
roaming through the hard cities, tough
himself as coffin nails.

Harping on the nettles of his melancholy,
keening on the blue strings of the blood,
he will delve into mythologies perhaps
call up spirits through the night.

Or carry memories apocryphal
of Tshaka, Hendrik Witbooi, Adam Kok,*
of the Xhosa nation's dream
as he moonlights in another country:

but he shall also have
cycles of history
outnumbering the guns of supremacy.

*Leaders of black resistance to white colonization

Now and wherever he arrives
extending feelers into foreign scenes
exploring times and lives,
equally may he stand and laugh,
explode with a paper bag of poems,
burst upon a million televisions
with a face as in a Karsh photograph,
slave voluntarily in some Siberia
to earn the salt of victory.

Darksome, whoever dies
in the malaise of my dear land
remember me at swim,
the moving waters spilling through my eyes:

and let no amnesia
attack at fire hour:
for some of us must storm the castles
some define the happening.

At Lansdowne Bridge

After the whoosh of doors slid shut
at Lansdowne Bridge I swim in echoes.
Who fouled the wall O people?
FREE THE DETAINEES someone wrote there.

Black letters large as life stare you
hard by day in the black face;
above the kikuye grass to the sandflats
goes the boorish clang-clang of railways.

Darkness neutralizes the request
till dawn falls golden and sweet,
though a sudden truck by night
cornering, holds it in spidery light.

Cosmos in London

Leaning over the wall at Trafalgar Square
we watch the spray through sun-drenched eyes,
eyes that are gay as Yeats has it:
the day suggests a photograph.
Pigeons perch on our shoulders as we pose
against the backdrop of a placid embassy,
South Africa House, a monument of granite.
The seeds of peace are eaten from our brown palms.

My friend in drama, his beady black eyes
in the Tally Ho saloon at Kentish Town:
we are exchanging golden syllables
between ensembles. I break off to applaud
a bourgeois horn-man. A fellow in a yellow
shirt shows thumbs up: men are demonstrative.
While big-eyed girls with half-pints stand
our minds echo sonorities of elsewhere.

One time he did Macbeth
loping across like a beast in Bloemfontein
(Othello being banned along with Black Beauty).
The crowd cheered, they cheered also
the witches, ghosts: that moment you could feel
illiteracy drop off them like a scab.
O come back Africa! But tears may now
extinguish even the embers under the ash.

There was a man who broke stone
next to a man who whistled Bach.
The khaki thread of the music emerged
in little explosions from the wiry bodies.
Entranced by the counterpoint
the man in the helmet rubbed his jaw
with one blond hand, and with the other
pinned the blue sky up under his rifle.

Tobias should be in London. I could name
Brutus, Mandela, Lutuli – but that memory
disturbs the order of the song, and whose
tongue can stir in such a distant city?
The world informs her seasons, and she,
solid with a kind of grey security,
selects and shapes her own strong tendencies.
We are here, nameless, staring at ourselves.

It seems at times as if I am
this island's lover, and can sing her soul,
away from the stuporing wilderness where
I wanted the wind to terrify the leaves.
Peach aura of faces without recognition,
voices that blossom and die bring need for death.
The rat-toothed sea eats rock, and who escapes
a lover's quarrel will never rest his roots.

Steve Chimombo

From Napolo

The Messengers

Napolo has spoken: Death.
The lizard scuttled in the undergrowth;
the excitement he carried did not burden him.
Mankind awaited his coming.

Napolo has spoken: Life.
The Chameleon stopped to consider
a joint in his leg and hesitated.
He rolled an eye behind and in front,
the shrubbery swallowed his form.
Mankind awaited his coming.

Napolo has spoken:
The man in the loincloth came to us at dawn.
We gathered round to hear the message,
but did not understand.
He spoke to us in a strange tongue
and we greeted it with laughter.
He turned his back on us;
now we shall never know.
And yet Napolo had spoken.

Obituary

He was a blessing one never prays for —
lightning coming uninvited
while men, women, and children flee
in terror at Mphambe's wrath;
but, once the god has struck
and buried his bolt in the earth,
they rush to the riven place,
claw at its charred remains,
if a tree, at its bark or splinters:
the closer to the thunderbolt,
the more potent the charm.

He was a gift one never utters thanks for —
locusts swarming after the planting rains
while men, women, and children watch
with desperate hearts and raging eyes,
their tender shoots ravished by a horde
of sharp teeth and clicking jaws;
but, once darkness has descended,
run to grab the drooping bodies
and bring home basketfuls of heaven-sent food
from the ravaged greenery after the guests
have laid waste the year's promise.

He stood among us, divine,
listening to our songs,
supervising the rain dances,
receiving our sacrifices
of bull, goat, or cock,
drinking to the dregs
prayers fermenting in beer.

We sang praisesongs:
He alone fought the *chidangwaleza*
that haunted the ancestral shrine.
He alone drank the *chilope* from its veins.
He alone shaved Changula's scales.

He sang his own refrains:
I know what broke the elephant's tusks
at the foot of the *dzaye* fruit tree.
I know what shrivelled the hair
from the old pheasant's head.
He met Napolo head-on.

Of Promises and Prophecy

PROLOGUE

Tomorrows reactivate somnolence
todays perpetuate inertia
yesterdays diffuse dismembered hopes:
the eternal miasma of zombies,

smeared in disco lights
lacerated with reggae sounds
groping in the darkness between
the tavern, bar, and rest house:

progress punctuated by puddles
of vomit, sweat, beer, and wine,
the whore's smile and the thug's
demand for a light or else.

I

No, they shall not have the truth
for facts are explosives
in anonymous brown bags
exploding between the fingers,
blowing reality into oblivion.

Let the few remaining honest souls
still roaming dangerously abroad
be lured again into the folds
of festering falsehood.

Let common knowledge become
the property of the minority
and mystification be manna
and hyssop for the masses.

And so, after taking some
for one or two rides
let us recede into the citadels
of silence and feed the people
with more lines of lies.

And under the shroud of silence
let retrospection unroll the map,
trace the tracks of introspection
to pinpoint where the derailment
and mass burial of truth took place.

II

No, don't jog memory anymore,
let it coil as harmless
as a puffadder until it's stepped upon,
only add more fuel to the amnesia,
programmed inertia and somnolence.

Let the few tumescent egos still around
mass-produce psychic onanism,
pack them into portable and compact
shapes that will fit into trunks, cases,
bags, pocket books, and passports
saleable at the next port of entry.

Educate the masses with new tools
of ideological bio-feedback
irrigate their drought-stricken spirits with
technological fried-while-you-starve
computerized mind-swopping, malaise,
anomy, and emotional dehydration.

Arm the beggars, vagrants, peasants
with transistorized pleas, canned laughter,
mesmerize the workers with videotaped leisure,
press-gang local witches into astronauts,
cauterize hope, desire, and memory.

Where are the great plans now?
Where the blueprints?
What is the programme?
What now?

EPILOGUE

Shall I destroy the citadel
and rebuild it in three days?
Three days in which will rise
a monolith of groans, gasps, and gashes
that are mouths screaming silent,
soul-searing, razor-sharp agony?

Three days in which will sprout
a luxurious green gold garden
with patches of marinas, mazdas,
fiats, fords, buicks, and benzes?

Armed with a multi-pronged plan
Man-Against-Self and Society (MASS)
I descended from the mountain top
with a blueprint of self-raising ideology,
improved-me conditions,
modern methods of mass-hypnosis,
and broke the citadels of silence.

Four Ways of Dying

The celebrants chanted
to the reluctant martyrs-to-be:
we would have a blood sacrifice!

The Crab's response:
I crawl
in my shell sideways,
            backwards,
            forwards
Avoid
      direct action on public matters,
      confrontation,
      commitment;
Meander
      to confuse direction or purpose,
                        meaning,
                        sense;

Squat
    to balance the issues,
    weigh,
    consider.

The Chameleon's answer:
Until I have exhausted my wardrobe,
lost my dye to a transparent nothingness,
free of reflection, true to my image,
I'll match my colours with yours,
snake my tongue out to your fears,
bare my teeth to puncture your hopes,
tread warily past your nightmares,
curl my tail round your sanctuaries,
clasp my pincer legs on your veins,
to listen to your heart beat.

The Mole's descent:
Wormlike I build in the entrails of the earth,
fashion intricate passages and halls,
tunnel utopias and underground Edens,
substitute surface with subterranean vision,
level upon level of meaning of existence,
as I sink downwards in my labyrinth,
to die in a catacomb of my own making.

The Kalilombe's ascent:
The gestation and questioning are over,
I'm restless with impatient foetuses,
belly-full with a profusion of conundrums.
My pilgrimage takes me to the cradle,
the *nsolo* tree, the lie-in of man's hopes.
I grit my teeth, grab the slippery surface
and hoist myself up the nation's trunk.
On the topmost branch I have momentary

possession of eternity whirling in the chaosis;
with the deathsong floating from my lips,
I fling myself down on Kaphirintiwa rock
as multivarious forms of art and life
issue out from the convulsions
of the ruptured womb;
and thus I die.

Derailment: A Delirium

I

I made the pilgrimage again
to the mountain top to divine
how Napolo parted the waters,
the granite, chunks of earth,
tree trunks, and the skies,
creating the cataclysms
in the mountain, the psyche, and hepatitis.

I drove past my grandmother,
skin stark black under the white dress,
owl glasses glinting in the sunlight,
as I tore past her, waving.
She waved back,
and I wept at ninety miles an hour
wondering: had she got hepatitis too?

On the mountain top
I parked at the end of the queue,
self-consciously inching my way
to the life-giving waters.
Started and stopped,
knowing the blockage had infected
the blood system, arteries, veins.

Started and stopped,
being careful not to disturb
migrant viruses and zombies.
Started and stopped.
Read a book, smoked, stared around
to count how many zombies
had gone before me,
how many were coming,
starting and stopping,
behind me, praying
I'd get there before
the sacred waters dried up.
Started and stopped.

II

I wanted to talk to the other suppliants
swirling around me like amoebas and viruses,
to deliberate the issues concerning the liver,
the causes and effects of the invasion,
and the blockage.

Faces:
maimers of my psyche.
Faces:
'These days I only go out with contractors.'

Faces:
'These girls are really decent
but I guess I'll never convince you.'

Snakes
who had abandoned sloughing
formed a corporation
and now make their own
wash 'n' wear fabrics.
Polecats
bought shares in industry
to increase the pollution explosion.
Crocodiles
swam upstream among the marshes
and launched a tears-by-the-gallon campaign.
Cultists,
infected by moral elephantiasis
(not hepatitis)
preached the brotherhood
of all zombies.

But queueing in a car
is not conducive
to contact and dialogue:
metal and glass walls
block communication and vision,
and all I meet are chromium-plated
forms swimming in exhaust fumes:
cabbage-lives wrapping timid centres,
peanut-in-pod existences,
eyes of zombies queueing
at the fountain of life.

III

Now indeed Leza has fled this land.
Only Mphambe reigns toying with man,
and Chiluwe, past master in subterfuge,
brings locusts to the table,
leaving the fields bare;
joy to the mouth,
grief to the soul;
peace to the stomach,
war to the mind.

I think as I start and stop:
wasn't it you grovelling
at the foot of the *nsolo* tree,
imploring Chauta to tell you
why Napolo had passed here?
Wasn't it you pouring
libations thrice to know
the meaning of the drought?

And should I not now
lift up the loincloth yet again
from the rafters and ascend the peak
to read from the granite-faced
rock of Kaphirintiwa
the meaning of hepatitis?

But Chiluwe had beaten me to the fountain,
he and his United Witches' Corporation
ganging on his side riding baskets,
hyenas' backs, owls' wings,
and the *nzulule's* night battle cry.

I paused in my stride:
had I come back to this?
Hepatitis?

Hepatitis,
that was my enemy
and I didn't know it.
Just think of it:
hepatitis was not across the border
but right here,
in the liver, within.

I ignored Chiluwe
and proceeded
unafraid
to the life-giving waters.

IV

Napolo spoke to me
in the waters regenerating my car:
'What kind of hepatitis, son?'
'Premium, please,' I said trembling.
And I saw hordes of them:
layer upon layer,
amoebas and viruses
debating what to do
with your liver.
Premium or Regular?
Amoebic or Viral?

What is hepatitis?
An administrator
wondering what web to spin
and how far across the room
it should reach?

How do you get hepatitis?
From friends speaking so close
you can count how many drinks
they had last night?

How can you tell the difference?
The colour of their eyes,
the palms or the soles of their feet,
a certain discolouration of the nails
tells they are not pedigree.

(And at night
I see your outline in the doorway;
see through to the liver blockage,
the bile flowing into the bloodstream
like petrol into my car.

Could you move
more certainly in the doorway
so I can see what you've got?
A or B Type?

You passed the doorway again
three times in one morning,
wearing hepatitis.
I asked at last, innocent-like:
each time you pass by
you have a different kind.
What kind is it this time?
Viral or Amoebic?
Premium or Regular?)

And I sat by the phone
getting messages from satellites,
wondering at the same time:
do satellites transmit hepatitis?
Operator, urgent, please,
I've got to talk to hepatitis.

V

At the fountain head I stopped and prayed:
Chauta, I want my kids, the nanny, her kid and sister,
the sixty-year-old man we call garden-boy,
all inoculated against hepatitis,
so their livers don't get blockages,
their biles don't flood the bloodstream,
so their conjunctivitis doesn't mix with their colds,
their diarrhoea, pinworm, and their arithmetic;
so they can sing the national anthem
in the garden as they play house;
so it doesn't interfere with their appetite
as they gather it, running, dancing, and riding
the only bike, it seems, in the neighbourhood;
so it doesn't pass on to the CCAP kids
who, after school, politely enough,
walk to the front door, in spite of the puppy:
could they please pluck off a few guavas
from the garden, they were hungry?
They are always hungry
since in the morning they visited
the tree without asking me.

Chauta, remember also, I told the kids
they could eat the guavas,
but to be careful with the hepatitis
flowering in the branches on the northern side.
It's infectious: up to six weeks for the incubation,
up to six months in bed.
No guavas, no school, no dancing, no anthem,
only hepatitis.

Remember, too, watching them go to the tree,
swarming in the branches, even the northern ones,
I wondered how long it would take
to reach their livers.

VI

And she came to me floating upon the waters,
limpid in her *chitenje* like an after-swim
spirit-maid of Mulungusi, among the amoebas,
swirling in the chaosis with the viruses.

Napolo spoke to me again above the roar:
'It's the friendly kind,' he said.
He'd give me some nice things
to think about instead of nightmares;
give me some nice things to do, too,
like letting me finger her liver,
trace the bile oozing its way up the arteries,
to see how far it had got.
Like letting me share her hepatitis,
for better or for worse.
And that's being nice, really.
When she comes home again
we can go for a second honeymoon
to a hepatitis-free cottage
by the lake.

She spoke to me through the fumes:
'It's no mystery at all, really,
only a blockage of the liver,
a fortuitous derailment of the bile
outside the borders of gamma globulin;
the blockage playing havoc with the arteries
that feed the nation: an influx of amoebas and viruses;
something to be laughed away at cocktail parties;
a parliament of amoebas and viruses
assembling in the hostels of our being,
sorting out our livers, rifling our bile,
to see how far we can survive amoeba rights
to live in our liver.
Parasites.
Viruses.'

She ended her message with the usual:
'See you soon, I hope.'
As in the old song, I said:
'In a while, hepatitis.'

A Death Song

(*Birimankhwe maso adatupa ninji?*
Kwathu maliro.
msamaseke ana inu:
kwayera mbee, mbee, mbee.

Ine n'dzachoka pam'dzi pano;
mutsale mumange pam'dzi pano.
Taonani pakhomo pangapa:
payera mbee, mbee, mbee.)

I

(Chameleon, why are your eyes swollen?
There's death at home.)

The Chameleon was wrong.
The tear-stricken swollen
swivelling eyes did not see
the lizard still scuttling
on the potsherds of Kaphirintiwa;
did not hear the Kalilombe's
survival song as she burst open
to give birth to laughter, song and dance.

Yes, the locusts came
and joined the army worms
and the monkeys in the middle
of the maize, bean and groundnut gardens;
but the west brought aids
and hybrid maize to replenish
the ravished sturdy local stock.
The east brought yaws too
in nice neat rice packets
and the media promised us
another bumper harvest because
of the prevailing peace and prosperity.

II

(*Look at my homestead.
it's empty, empty, empty.*)

The Chameleon was wrong.
The homestead was not really empty.
Some zombies were left
in spite of their deafness.
The *ndondochas* wailed at night
despite their tongues being cut off.
They were not yet completely dead.

Yes, carloads of souls
met their sticky ends
at the end of the line.
However, the survivors were permitted
to attend the funerals and burials
under careful supervision.

III

(*I shall leave this village;
you stay behind and build this village.*)

The Chameleon was wrong.
The answer was not to abandon the village
as rats do a sinking ship
or fleas a dying hedgehog.
Exile, pretended, genuine,
or self-imposed is not the answer
to the holocaust or the apocalypse.

Yes, we seek new homes everyday,
the old ones no longer habitable.
We hunt for new myths everywhere
the ancient ones defaced or defiled.
However, recycled myths or homes
are better than nothing,
they are all we have left.

IV

(*Do not laugh, children:*
it's empty, empty, empty.)

You are wrong, Chameleon.
Just look at the survivors:
how many Nyanjas did not hurtle
headlong into Chingwe's Hole?
How many Ngonis did not
partake of the *Kalongonda?*
How many Chewas were not
crushed at Mpata-wa-Milonde?
How many Kafulas did not
suffocate in the Bunda caves?
How many Tumbukas staved off
starvation on Hora Mountain?

Yes, you are wrong, Chameleon.
Just count how many delayed
their deaths in spite of the lizard's message.
Look how laughter, song, and dance
still rebound against the rock
of Kaphirintiwa:
we are still alive!

Jack Mapanje

Messages

1

Tell her we still expose our bottoms
Eat unseasoned *nsima* with *bonongwe*
From a wooden ladle our hands unscented,
We still sleep in slums rolling
In bird-droppings, friends of fleas,
Maggots. Tell her our pleasure
Is still in the pattering tin-drums
That convoke these tatters in the cold
Of dawn to quench hangovers. Tell
Her besides, a cat sees best at night
Not much at noon and so when time
Comes, while she eats and drinks
While she twists and shouts, rides
And travels, we shall refuse
To reach her our stuff of fortune
Even if she called us witches!
We swear by our fathers dead!

2

The red neon light illuminates
Her loose butterfly skirt
The iron rippled hair
Her pink veneer smile

Her moist hand grips mine
Her forefinger goring my palm
What . . . ? She . . . ? – nail varnish
On my palm . . . 'a beer please . . . '

Her back swirls off me
Gassed by reeking perfumes, sitting:
Tattering curtains, doors to bathrooms
Couples in corners unabashed

She comes back thick-lip-cigaretted
The chest jutting into the world generously
The lashes greased bluer
'Come from far . . . ? Tired . . . eh . . . ?'

I reply a struck-Portuguese-match laughter
As I try to whisper her navel name
'Asawilunda, your mother at Kadango greets you and . . . '
Oh, already floating to the next customer?

3

Did you think it was a hunting party
Where after a fall from chasing a hare
You laughed together an enemy shaking
Dust off your bottom, a friend reaching
You your bow and arrow? Or a game safari
Where you patted your hounds before
The halloo? Did you think this the bush
Where the party would take the best of
Their kill to the Chief so he could allow
Them more hunting bush next time? No,
Mother, it's a war here, a lonely war
Where you hack your own way single-handed
To make anything up to the Shaka of
The tribe! It's fine the earth's fertile!

The Cheerful Girls at Smiller's Bar, 1971

The prostitutes at Smiller's Bar beside the dusty road
Were only girls once in tremulous mini-skirts and oriental
Beads, cheerfully swigging Carlsbergs and bouncing to
Rusty simanje-manje and rumba booming in the juke-box.
They were striking virgins bored by our Presbyterian
Prudes until a true Presbyterian came one night. And like
To us all the girls offered him a seat on cheap planks
In the dark backyard room choked with diesel-oil clouds
From a tin-can lamp. Touched the official rolled his eyes
To one in style. She said no. Most girls only wanted
A husband to hook or the fruits of Independence to taste
But since then mini-skirts were banned and the girls
Of Smiller's Bar became 'ugly prostitutes to boot!'

Today the girls still giggle about what came through
The megaphones: the preservation of our traditional
et cetera . . .

These Too Are Our Elders

Watch these elders. They always come at night
In bloated plumage, tossing you on their
Avocado noses, inhaling all the free air out
Of you. Their masks carry fatal viruses.

One came the other night draped in hyena skins
His face showing amid the fluffed out ostrich
Feathers, twisting his sinews in a frenzied
Dance. At work I was unseating him, he preached.

But I too went to the village he had visited.
They said I should ask him next time why
He always came at night, why he pretended
I was more useful than the Whiteman once in

My seat, and why he sent me to school at all?
Well, he merely backslid through the bamboo rafters
Showering behind rotten amulets and mice shit!
Why do these elders always exploit our disbelief?

On African Writing (1971)

You've rocked at many passage rites, at drums
Mothers clapping their admiration of your
Initiation voices – now praises of decay
That still mesmerize some; at times you've
Yodled like you'd never become men gallant
Hunting, marrying, hating, killing. But
In your masks you've sung on one praise
After another. You have sung mouth-songs!
Men struggling to justify what you touched
Only, heard merely! Empty men! Do you realise
You are still singing initiation tunes?
You have not chimed hunting-marrying –
Fighting-killing praises until you've
Stopped all this nonsense about drinking
Palm wine from plastic tumblers!
And these doggerels, these sexual-tribal
Anthropological-political doggerels!
Don't you think even mothers will stop
Quaking some day? Don't you realise
Mothers also ache to see their grand
Children at home playing *bau* on sofas?
Why do you always suppose mothers
Never want to see you at these conferences
They are for ever hearing about?
Why do you imagine they never understand
Things? They too can be alert to all this
Absurdity about what you think they think!
You've sung many songs, some superb
But these lip-songs are most despicable!

From Florrie Abraham Witness, *December* 1972

There are times when their faith in gods
Really fascinates me. Take when the Anglican
Priest with all pomp and ceremony married
Abraham and Florrie, why didn't he realise
Abe and Florrie would eventually witness
The true Jehovah in his most pristine? And silly
Little Florrie, couldn't she foresee the run against
The only cards possible when she said her
'Yes, I do; for kids or for none?' And when
Florrie's mother dear, with all her Anglican
Limping love for her first and only daughter
Still intact, even when she thought she might
Still visit the prodigals nothwithstanding, how
Couldn't she see that she too would be booted out
Landing carelessly bruised and in *Moça-*
mbique! The buggers! They surely deserve it;
They deserve such a good kick on their bottom.
I mean, there are times when their faith just
Fails me. Take today, when silly little Florrie
Should scribble a funny epistle on stupid roll –
And Love did you have to call it thus? I mean,
It sounds so strangely imprudent of . . . But . . .
Anyway: Darling Brother, only God of Abraham
Knows how we escaped the petrol and matches
Yet we are all in good hands. They give us
Free flour, beans free and their kind of salted
Meat and fish. We've even built a ten-by-ten yard
Little hospital for our dear selves. Only we
Haven't got any soap. But we'll manage and do not
Be anxious over us here dear Brother; Mummie
And the kids are all in good shape. They send
Their Christmas greetings. Read well and, oh, note:
Psalms! Where in London is the blooming Bible?

Glory Be to Chingwe's Hole

Chingwe's Hole, you devoured the Chief's prisoners
Once, easy villagers decked in leopard colours
Pounding down their energies and their sight.
You choked minstrel lovers with wild granadilla
Once, rolling under burning flamboyant trees.

Do you remember Frog the carver carving Ebony Beauty?
Do you remember Frog's pin on Ebony Beauty's head
That brought Ebony to life? And when the Chief
Heard of a beauty betrothed to Frog, whose dogs
Beat up the bushes to claim Ebony for the Chief?

Even when Fly alarmed Frog of the impending hounds
Who cracked Fly's bones? Chingwe's Hole, woodpeckers
Once poised for vermillion strawberries merely
Watched fellow squirrels bundled up in sacks
Alive as your jaws gnawed at their brittle bones.

Chingwe's Hole, how dare I praise you knowing whose
Marrow still flows in murky Namitembo River below you?
You strangled our details boasting your plush dishes,
Dare I glorify your rope and depth epitomizing horror?

Making Our Clowns Martyrs
(or Returning Home Without Chauffeurs)

We all know why you have come back home with no
National colours flanking your black mercedes benz.
The radio said the toilets in the banquet halls of
Your dream have grown green creepers and cockroaches
Which won't flush, and the orders you once shouted
To the concubines so mute have now locked you in.
Hard luck my friend. But we all know what currents
Have stroked your temper. You come from a breed of
Toxic frogs croaking beside the smoking marshes of
River Shire, and the first words you breathed were
Snapped by the lethal mosquitoes of this morass.
We knew you would wade your way through the arena
Though we wondered how you had got chosen for the benz.
You should have been born up the hills, brother where
Lake waters swirl and tempers deepen with each season
Of the rains. There you'd see how the leopards of
Dedza hills comb the land or hedge before their assault.
But welcome back to the broken reed-fences, brother;
Welcome home to the poached reed-huts you left behind;
Welcome to these stunted pit-latrines where only
The pungent whiff of buzzing green flies gives way.
You will find your idle ducks still shuffle and fart
In large amounts. The black dog you left still sniffs
Distant recognition, lying, licking its leg-wounds. And
Should the relatives greet you with nervous curiosity
In the manner of masks carved in somebody's image,
There is always across the dusty road, your mad auntie.
She alone still thinks this new world is going shit.
She alone still cracks about why where whys are crimes.

We Wondered About the Mellow Peaches

So, behind the heavy backyard orchard
And your generous invitations Alberto
To guava tart today and mango pudding tomorrow
Behind the spate of those Chilobwe township
Lambs brutally chopped in their dark huts
Where even undertakers dare not tread,
                                    There
Were whiskers, Alberto, to map the moves
And pay the bills? Why, why did waste my
Melodious song excoriating parochial squirrels
And hammerheads for readily running messages
Up and down bowing peachtrees and bringing
Flashy girls with mellow peaches and vermilion
Strawberries into lascivious range-rovers?
I should have erected them an edifice instead
I should have set up votive slabs from Mphunzi
Hills, chalked the rude walls with gentle
Gazelles and the lore about sweet foundlings—
To while away my temper. And yet, how could
The chameleon have lost grip of his own colours?
And did we need the restive decade to uncover
The plot? And this fuss about conspiracies and goats,
Didn't we all wonder about the mellow peaches?

Another Fools' Day touches down: shush

For Mercy, Judith, Lunda and Lika

Another Fools' Day touches down, another homecoming.
Shush. Bunting! some anniversary: they'll be preoccupied.
Only a wife, children and a friend, probably waiting.

A Ph.D., three books, a baby-boy, three and half years-
Some feat to put us . . . Shush. Such frivolities no longer
Touch people here. 'So, you decided to come back, eh?'

Rhetorical questions dredge up spastic images. Shush.
In the dusty, brown-grey landscape, the heat unrolls.
Some wizard has locked up his rainbows and thunder again.

Why do the gods hold up the rains?
Don't we praise them enough?
Shush. There are no towers here, no domes or gothic windows.
Only your children, friends, nestling up for a warm story.

Kojo Laing

Senior lady sells garden eggs

I love the lit corners of your kerosine smile,
your sympathy soft as new-boiled nkontommire
no whines come between you and this world, and
your large elbows take all the knocks possible. O
senior lady sits in the rain, sells
garden eggs with a sense of grace
under a wide hat wider than all my markets,
and the chewing-stick brushes
memories long dry with their own strength.
She meets life's one-wheel screams
with the subtlest roars in the land:
if you can't stop the rain
you can throw your own water up, or
store the biggest tank underground. Can
I too not give my floods direction, as
I watch you watch the deaths go by,
      watch the children grow like sugar-cane,
hard and sweet with your own dying.
I love the quiet corn boiling
as you look through its steam to far worlds,
your mind in a maze it loves, in prayers
spread on the waters like boats broad and dry.
Senior Lady sells garden eggs,
fights in her own way only when she must, and
she must; a slight almost hidden glint, in her eye,
            a tightening of the shoulders,
            a face set like shield or armour.

The water is flowing, stand back, you
can't be hard to a hard world forever, and
the great face shines
like the sun through morning mist, and strangely
the rain is caught in her large hands and sent home.

Godhorse

The horse with birds on its mane, doubt on its tail . . .
doubt about the flies being whisked north or south . . .
crawled out of the relieved horizon, in
a burst of dung part-coloured with kente.
And the angle at which the horse bisected the hills,
made it easy for the old man with the square body
to jump up its decorated left flank, leaving
half his age behind as his bones came down like a pounder.
Galloping was a definition of time, more
for the man, less for the horse
whose high brown snorting would be framed
if only there were strong hands,
if only the ancestors would jump the centuries.
Now a woman raised her right breast on the right flank
of this horse of wonder, this horse
with a mane maimed by the limiting beauty of birds.
Mansa's whole body shook – O god of soft thunder! –
as the old man stretched his lust across horse flesh,
trying to speed through the geography of tails, but
suddenly meeting ghana
                              half-way up the horse instead; suddenly
seeing bishops and fetish priests
so that his reverence gently covered his lust, true
the religious men wanted to bless the impudent hooves, but

the horse threw off angels with a burst of shank, with
the old man kneeling on the saddle and begging Mansa for love,
as her breasts shook in incense.
Since the sun and moon were
                in a simultaneous sky,
Mansa watched half a country hand on half a horse,
                watched the old man's smiles and rejected
                        each one,
throwing the most outrageous one under the hardest hoof.
Pound your laughter, pound your world!
Rejection was no different, even when mixed with speed,
old man's nails were digging into horse country,
old man's knees were shaking the shanks
                of a suddenly stationary stallion:
horse hair was full of brown regret,
                was full of the morality of not galloping
when the country was sagging with the speed of time.
But let horse dung salute accra!
Let the blue moon burst over a clear gallop!
Let them rise against the unwanted pity of horse ethics!
We want the african touch, neighed the horse, for
it desperately loved Mansa's thighs pressing against it. But
old man shouted the horse on. Onnnn!
For the half of ghana that was missing
                was merely the gaps in his old teeth,
                was merely the spatial side of galloping.
On! Human flesh orbits horse flesh!
Old man falls from flank to flank,
bouncing across a withering country, shivering
under the weight of horse decrees
                that Mansa carried on behalf of the
                        authorities.
On! with the most moral horse in the world, for its
thighs did not return the pressure of Mansa's thighs, for

after all the universe was a stilled gallop,
> was an old man crawling away from a
> > cantering, crazy life,
> was a contradictory shank shaking.
As Mansa fell off at last by the tune of a distant highlife,
the horse snorted for other women, the
> horse . . . its morality lost in its speed at last . . .
> > threw off the old man.
Man, poor, old: he died with a smile before he hit the ground:
> > and under him were the crushed birds, O God,
> > carrying their expanding beauty still, still.

Africa sky

The wind of old cocoa farms
> makes the war song of the storm.
What can I do with fifty trees
whose roots are bared in the rain?
Small rivers shoot through
small grass and small joys,
> like the hands of girls outstretched
> > strongly yawning.
> Africa is handled in a dance.
Now the rain falls gently in sloping L's
into my surname and my trees,
> beyond flowers bending into moving mud.
Once in the storm,
> Africa is handled in a dance by lost girls,
who meet to make my thoughts wander
into places where roots are suddenly
> fewer than the threats that bind them.
And song with salt be sung,

to make rivers seas I wash in.
The rain falls in shouts which do not slope,
for the farms bend for the skies.
   Roots are the teeth of earth bared
in the brown ground of girls,
whose dancing hands take this country
and throw it into the clear skies there,
      near the stream of my unwashed hopes.
         Africa is handled in a dance
               by lost girls with the sky in their eyes!

Tatale Swine

Tatale there rounding the fat woman that fried it,
long life to the evening in the police station, where
the sunset spread into the inspector's eyes,
so that rays covered the law with tremendous streaks,
eyes so hard that you could stamp a thief's foot in it. Swine!
One police boot was beyond the universe, for
as it walked in the rain it did not get wet:
the swing that swung the boot marched the rain away,
and the sergeant moved under the snarl of his stripes,
under the zoo-bars of the room all-correct-sir, spoken
from a mouth stiff with the waakyi of its phrase, so
that as the children marched in their dance, walk, dance,
accra had the smoothest movement in sunset.
Attention to the corned-beef sky under which the police ate!
for every mouth chewed Independence and the future:
the loaf of the map of ghana had many bites missing, and
the bad and bitter biter was never seen.
The prisoner yawned to attention, dividing
his life among the indivisible, wiping his nose

with sly salutes to the police.
And he said: he was charger and charged, a
            failure with Highlife in his teeth,
                was guilty of letting onions rot in his hands,
and he promoted itches on unscratchable backs. Swine!
Into the matches the sergeant took his fingerling sorrow,
walking about with a national frown, wailing
that the deepest compound he could sweep
was only of the stone of the police, sharing
his smoke between his lung and his country. Swine!
to the sunset that attacked the inspector's eyes,
to the arresting rays that framed him, moved
a yard of sky to make way for the moon.
And the truth of its light travelled the cap,
pressed an inch of sunset out of the eye.
And the prisoner caught the falling rays, shouting:
I have this law of light
to let you see what we really are, my
real moon shines a fraud on the roots.
Swine! The sergeant roared: don't talk your craze!
Today was two days: one for the long glow of uniforms,
one for the short spirit of the country,
and the inspector saluted the thinning sky, glad
for the darkness as the clouds pressed on light.
The children marched out of the future,
and someone stepped on the moon's past,
for there were police boots upside-down in the sky
but wearing the feet of all in the country.
At last the woman rose gauging her kerosine,
putting her own shape slowly into the tatale,
moving her light far from the evening
as the prisoner watched the shape expand.
The sergeant shared the guilt in his waakyi,
and what couldn't they share, the police, the people,
when the moon itself was mean with light? Swine!

I am the freshly dead husband

I am the freshly dead husband,
I write my death to a fashionable wife:
Dear Dede with the new-bought guarantees, Dede
with the obsession to push hurriedly some
shared memories into my crowded box, crowded
with the two parts of me that were still alive:
    brain and popylonkwe
        still vibrant above the desolation of my other parts,
           above the rotting of my stylish wrists.
I was not properly dead,
I could hear you chat prettily as I lay in state . . .
        and what a state, involving an accident
          with a supertobolo girlfriend still alive . . .
with a funeral cloth of the best style, paid
from the breathless anticipation of my retiring benefits.
Boxes and benefits, hearts and betrayal, ginnnnn!
        How can you mourn me!
To shed tears you had to borrow
from the sorrow of your father's funeral
held last year, when I couldn't cry.
Together my actions and your inventions pushed
all grief to the children who,
not knowing any better, loved my carefree syncopations.
Dede with the black-brown eyes
        whose shades were deeper in the left eye, I
salute your show of courageous grief when
you convinced my mother of the authenticity of your tears!
Bless you, your grief was becoming so successful
that you were, with decorum, fantastically enjoying my death.
I am dead but hungry for guavas . . .
I foolishly imagined the rainbow,
                with its inappropriate joy,
torn from a sky that never gave me any sign till I was dead.

Dede, don't let them push my hearse so fast, have
a little posthumous consideration
                    for my erection of the after-life:
a dead man can't go to God with his popylonkwe at attention.
God forgive your speed
for you want to disgrace me before the ancestors!
Hurrying to bury me . . .
hey wait, the erection still stands . . .
was the horror for my mother, whose
tears, so bewildered, could not quite reach me
                    in my wooden flagless castle . . . she
was beginning to sense a picnic atmosphere,
demure girls danced in their walk by my grey skin
                    now spiritual at last, at last.
                    And I wish my funeral would panic!
Dede I agree I often betrayed you, usually
just at the point when you were
                    simultaneously betraying me, I
imprisoned you in my successes and excesses,
I took your gin and doubled it.
As I speak these words,
fresh ants crawl over me with their white eggs, I
noiselessly knock and bite my coffin! for
it is too tight for me to wear, I need a different size!
Dede, help me, I demand air-conditioning, I need
the coolness now that you never gave me! But
your back is turned, you adjust your duku in the mirror.
You look in great fashion by my rotting chin.
Did you really have to try so hard
to stop yourself from laughing, as
you realised that I was dreaming
about being buried next to that girl that I REALLY loved!??

And she did burst out laughing as the last dust covered me . . .
And her laughter said: I was truthful about all my boxed lies.
Yes, but I will write again!
I see the ginnnnn of resurrection glass to glass!

The same corpse

     Nothing can be done about the rain in your meal.
It's a wrong thing to train so much light on fufu, for
the governments suspended on the finest mortars,
suffer the Ghana pestles just for the taste
of being pounded into amazingly tasty food, with
abenkwan brightened by different lights
        distinguished by different mouths, for
the pounded man is the pounded country.

*

The governments suspended on the finest mortars,
use cranes to extract sharp bad teeth,
shiver at parties with Fufu Decrees, lengthen
the legs of beautiful girls just by stretching regions,
stretching the bones of graveyards
               that grow younger and younger
                 every year,
so that in an interdependent world, the
inter does not belong to Ghana.

*

To suffer the Ghana pestles just for the taste
is to make wasted pain out of history, for
the committees that march on the problems of the country,
are footless toeless and legless, but
use the most wonderful boots that move automatically
into all the ministerial seas that drown them. Yet,
    and yet and yet
again the political man rises with a weird roar at the sea,

*

and nothing can be done about the rain in your meal, for
when Kofi Mensah was arrested Ama did it, and
when Ama was arrested Kofi Mensah did it, freeeeeee!
so that Ghana is lost between bitter and sweet,
witches wail into the most stylish bones,
and we are back to the dog biting the country, and
the country biting the dog, but
sadly the tooth of the nation was finishing,

*

for the dog just laughed with
    the fastest jaws ever barked in mamprobi.
And after all Ghana had now received a contract
to export as much pure movement
as the magnificent buttocks of city alombos can create.
The Marketing Board For Projecting The Soul of Ghanaians
moved impurely, danced to stagnant laws, so
that the distinction of different mouths was a saltless
    abenkwan.

*

And the pounded man is the pounded country,
arrest me-O, don't arrest me-O
I will still live below your politics, cutting
the roots whenever I can, burning the pride with the ironies
    of history.
You cry I laugh, you laugh I cry, and
when the flag was upside down, no one noticed,
for the amazingly tasty fufu
    had finally shrivelled the jaws that ate it.

*

O they dance! One rotten back matches another. It's
wrong to train so much light on this fufu, for
dogs are busy releasing fleas into the beauty left. Dance!
to the rhythms of mass bands massively wrong, and
brightened by different lights
the different shames suffer under Ghana pestles.
On Kofi, On! You are brilliant! You
and I are trying to kill the same corpse! Ewurade!

Many worlds are walked once

The dogs bark ably: in Accra
one bark stiffens ten strangers, and
sets the malaria in the teeth chattering; another
bark fiercely gathering baritone, conducts
the storm in its jaws to the storm in the clouds.
The many legs of dogs walk one world.
Even in the evening
when wise journeys have come to an end, and
she spreads her own cries of alarm
around my sleeping head,
all other sounds are echoes from the tongues of dogs,
and the love she speaks I cannot hear,
for it has its own language,
which the dogs and I want to burst through:
dogs hate giving their echoes to love,
and I don't want to be the man at the end of a doubtful bite,
with only alternate teeth in love.
The pattern of one stranger's spit
has confused the confident dogs:
the saliva of orchestral barking
matches the stranger's mouth,
which spits only incidentally:
barking at thieves and cursing the world create the same
saliva.
And the dogs are able to bark in Accra
merely because the lovers have all hoarded their love,
so that one loveless bark stiffens ten hearts, and
the breasts that could be stupendous with my handling
are now lazily moved around the city
by her reluctant shoulders.
And so to the storm with the jaws missing!
Rain beats dogs, rain roars against the barking

which is already weak with the love of our shared doubt,
        is already going tenor now
          as the fierceness softens in the storm.
And so the thunder!
neutral with its own force, scattering
strangers, dogs, hearts and echoes,
yet keeping us together
by wakening me with a meditated clap of aerial slapping, so
that in the absence of barking
I push your breasts away from the sudden lightning,
        from electric love.
Many worlds are walked once by dogs' legs,
many worlds hold us half,
the voices of many strangers drown your language,
and all I can see in the rain,
             in the evenings of wisdom when
             we are quiet,
is your unscattered heart carrying its own words, and
pushing me away from its hoard of alarmed love.
                  Storm!
                  I say storm!

One hundred lines for the coast

Grown old are these strong elements of tragedy,
the strength the elephant's head brings to a whole country,
bright centuries of betrayal for a noon of funerals,
and the dead in their dramatic drums and dances,
congregating in deserted beaches full of the roars
    of sorrow,
and these broad cliffs holding the sea in granite embrace,
touching redeemed countries amazed and tired far beyond
    the shores,
slicing the receding silence with large harmonies
    large death,
and all the commotion of histories deeper for being
    beyond discovery,
all the rhythm of time trapped in giant webs, terrible
    and kind,
and grown old without wisdom by generations of dire
    disconnection.
The calmest hands mould marred houses of grace
    and inconsequence
old sea rites come at death, forgotten forests advance
    in meaning,
spread their leaves higher than all the faith for tomorrow,
and patterns of prophets storm a sky of humid and
    broken hopes,
along ridges of transformed visitations and secular
    intensity,
Gods live and laugh with us all on horizons hidden
    with palm-trees,
this is where we live this is where we die with our dreams
of fires that sustain the dance where flesh never burns
but becomes bright dark and beautiful with all the Ananse
    deception here,
all the primal shame that breaks into eternal groping,

and this, and this is the song of a country wild for
    peace and ritual.
The sea lies in the moon, cries to the fury
    of its own waves,
and the towns come, great cargoes in their gutters green,
the colourful spirit shrinks into the smallest
    beer-bottles,
the streets generate their own energy of ampe
and hurry feet and wheels nowhere but everywhere,
and the red dust marks the footsteps on the bofrot sun,
and the touching is tired the dancing is dreary and
    distant,
all this spirit is but a scream in the storm unheard,
    strange
and stranger for the peace that turns a corner
    sharp and bewildered,
where tiger-nuts chewed make the chatter innocent
    and scattered,
fine faces weary with beauty, the break of dawn
    and laughter and sin
over us under us through the sanest souls in the plains.
Neem trees drive hard roots into sly sewers of mercy,
    searching,
Searching for the song of amputated hospitals
    forever unhealing,
The song of fetish priests with their tremolos of man,
    woman and money,
The song of akpeteshie, of villages of night-singing
    and night-telling,
of rich soups and sacrificial yam, wide songs and subtle bodies,
beyond the swagger of herbal cities of mud and steel,
    gutters and incense,
all the song of a people bursting
and punching for the harvests of history,
and the grasses rise in the savannas, the flamboyants rise,

the roses rise,
and the zoos rise in the forests, adowa groups rise,
      chiefs raise their rhythms,
the trotro is raised, the adinkra cloth is raised, gravestones
raise their wails to God, He answers in the deepest
      fontomfroms of thunder.
The saddest souls rise with the sun everyday
      and every death,
majestically ruined feeder roads still at war with
      dying lorries, high
tears flow in the dance of birth, hundreds of bishops
      hide their holiness,
the country grins to fair nuns of bacon and suffering,
      priests
take their mercedes in beautiful kilometres of oware
      to heaven high,
the universe vomits and hemispheres flow into
      fresh palm-wine,
into the circular sorrows of thieves dead by the
      hands of peaceful people,
mallams bless the toenails of important people,
      snails ban abenkwan,
and it is hard to grip the great reefs in a hug
      of matrimony,
it is hard to free dead time from ludo and rumours,
      football and fame,
fair and foul, Easter picnics, no time and all time, foul.
Who creates the symmetry here, who lays hands
      on the dancing breasts?
Who tames the poets become pundits and showmen running
      like gari?
Eyes beady like taxis, the dawn tames a sleeping country,
cremated kelewele tames a burning country, and the soil
      is compassion,
elephants ice their foreheads to charge a hard country,

and in the funeral plains children know all about death,
   yet
keep the generations going with their laughter
   and timeless silences,
and we are alive with the insects, this juju of surprise
   is dead,
you roof your building, you roof your soul,
   you roof your country,
small choirs sing in disembodied discord,
   beauties spiritual and
disproportionate, in harmony. Her moist lips sing
   halleluja, Yes.
The poor man rises with courage, faces the darkest
   drains of inner pain,
when you die your cloth will be beautiful your rings
   shining,
your rhythms have no time, only patterns and breaks
   profound,
only the sweat I shed by the heart in corners
   of dementation,
only the long fight with powers wet with canoes
   of their own pushing
will save these cliffs, these towers, these mosques,
with the soft voice passing through a hard country
   of the palm-nut head,
penny bicycles, bofrots in sieves, HighLife boogie-woogie
horses with their afterthoughts of dung, stylish mammies
   of woe and welcome:
they are some of the spirits at the gates, but which
dam will hold still all the wealth of this tragic river?
And aeroplanes get stuck dragging fresh clouds
   to the savannas,
and the four corners of the Coast are the feet
   of angry elephants,
and the wild rain is the tears of those yet to be born, and

of proverbs dying,
tears and laughter mixed in angular beauty
    more profound than machines,
and every country has its own complacencies
    of the spirit,
its own sad and original versions of betrayal,
    of the chewing-gum of the soul,
of sewers of pain where rats are artful kings
    articulate with death,
the moon falls in the sea, gods get grievous
    in mysterious ridges,
and the whole world is fufu, and the soup is my death,
    is your death,
withered forests, pot-holes in highways,
    unanswered petitions,
all tragedies grown old before the meeting of elders.
And all the dead in their dramatic drums and dances,
congregating in deserted beaches full of the roars
    of sorrow,
I salute all your pain, I drum the cathedrals
    of your tragedy,
I cram your hands into this sympathy unwanted,
I create your peace with the quietest roars
    in the market-places!
And in all dead Hail to your hot and granite
                                        Mysteries.

Race on Gathering Bites

Air-borne ants attacked softer parts of cyclist, measuring
each bite in fast metres, each pain in slow miles,
so that ants and speed
              made a whole in a world crawling with bites . . . but
nice to know the popylonkwe was excluded.
The grip on his flesh was also on his thinking
that a quick fistful of black ants thrown at the horizon
made a face of God grimacing
through the riding and biting of insects
created in a moment of inspired crawling, for
the rest of the heavens were anti-ant, anti-crawl.
He raised the momentum of pedalling, thrusting
his moist neck under the breezes, pushing
out the hope that the wind would whirl the ants down,
or at least disengage the bites which
now took on more meaning than the biters themselves.
Teeth and speed were something philosophical, were
rushing to contradict the calm spaces between bites,
so that he as the cyclist could not
dispute the march of time merely by stopping.
Race on gathering bites! even to your death, for
pincers thus charged could be instruments
for implementing aspects
                       of the last judgment of ghana:
                       we have eschatological wheels.
Race on! for after all, the togetherness of ants
was an indictment
of the eternal brokenness of human beings,
was tough on all the Mensahs of the world!
We push forward into the breeze of teeth, we
create noise at a corner by
              screaming against all the bites of love.
So he cycles on, loving his own contortions, making

comedy from a heart broken by a thousand actions, for
the back-tyre reached the zenith
    of its own revolutions by
wishing to be still below the silliest screaming . . .
it would make love to the front wheel,
if only they could touch above the pain,
two wheels feeling their own wind, only . . .
Finally he stopped to make a tremendous howl, for
he felt the last ant bite the last skin, so
that his swollen body was slowly turning into spirit.
Consciousness was a bitten body disappearing,
        was God's face ungrimacing,
was a revolving half-hidden scream
presented to a city that swore that ants and screams did not
                                   exist koraa.

The huge car with the sad voice

    The huge car with the sad voice
      has killed a chicken
  under the brown window with the trees
  whose leaves are her green eyes moving
      in the expectation of the breeze.

She sits in the rising dust,
surrounded by cashew-nuts
        and a smile from another heart.
Some tall laughing she used
to cook the chicken for someone,
talking idly, yet intensely ready
to fall in love when it doesn't hurt.

He said:
>the way you cook chicken bones
>glorifies the killing,
>you woman of okros and lavender.

she said, verifying his fear
with the pointed questions of her breasts.
She adjusted her eyes for the same love this time,
and then ran away from what she saw:

>>shallow love for a woman still searching.

The two white doors of two buildings
make unseen meaning around her,
emphasising what dreams she takes to his trees.
She was only prepared to gather
his words if she could bury them later.
>THERE
>she was with a hard hold of the heart, and
>with a strong will to reshape
>>her heart for her own sad life.
And she is slyly and strongly filled
>with the memories
>>of what she would have liked to become.
But who would have been surprised
>that she sat in that very same car
>that killed the chicken so carelessly
>>under the brown window with the trees,
her eyes going round and round, faster than the wheels under
>>>her . . .

Niyi Osundare

Excursion

Past bush paths tarred by tireless treading
Past rocky outcrops rubbed smooth by stubborn heels
Past dandelions roaring silently at my wandering feet
Past elephant grass fluted tusklessly by the wind.

Past the depleted copper of harvested cornfields
Past the leafy grove of ripening yams
Past the groundnut's leguminous lilt
in the orchestra of swinging furrows
Past the bean which has a thousand children
with antimony in each eye

Past the gallant butterfly dallying from flower to flower
Past the bee droning and dreaming in the hammock
of fallowing farms
Past the dung-beetle rolling in its forbidden ball
Past soldier ants bootless in their lengthy columns

Past the lake lying namelessly in the register
of famous shrubs
Past the duck which brailles liquid letters
on its open face
Past boulders and pebbles which answer the whisper
of calling feet
Past the quivering arrow of a noonward sun

Homeward
with a flower in one hand
Homeward
with a sun in the other
Homeward
To a house of sunful fragrance.

Who says that drought was here?

With these green guests around
Who says that drought was here?

The rain has robed the earth
in vests of verdure
the rain has robed an earth
licked clean by the fiery tongue of drought

With these green guests around
Who says that drought was here?

Palms have shed the shroud of brown
cast over forest tops
by the careless match of tinder days
when flares flooded the earth
and hovering hawks taloned the tale
to the ears of the deafening sky

With these green guests around
Who says that drought was here?

Aflame with herbal joy
trees slap heaven's face
with the compound pride
of youthful leaves

drapering twigs into groves
once skeletal spires in
the unwinking face of the baking sun

With these green guests around
Who says that drought was here?

And anthills throw open their million gates
and winged termites swarm the warm welcome
of compassionate twilights
and butterflies court the fragrant company
of fledgeling flowers
and milling moths paste wet lips
on the translucent ears of listening windows
and the swallow brailles a tune
on the copper face of the gathering lake
and weaverbirds pick up the chorus
in the leafening heights . . .
soon crispy mushrooms will break
the fast of venturing soles

With these green guests around
Who still says that drought was here?

eyeful glances

The desert caller
comes on a camel
of clouds,
undulates through the dunes
of hazy shadows
        &
gliding through the open welcome
of January's door
whispers urgent tidings
in the ears of my skin

*

a few teasing drops
on earth's gaping lips
vanishing like droplets
on a steel plate
hot with the forge's red rage

*

a tree leaflets the sprawling lawn
the grass reads between the veins
and up they rise
against trampling feet
borrowing anthems from the whistling wind.

*

a timid rain peeps behind the clouds
then recoils
abandoning the world
to the gruelling heat
of a hungry season

*

a parting cloud
grips the trigger
of a homing day
the sun bursts out
in a staccato
of orange idioms

*

the flame tree
coifs the forest
in petals of fire
(it's the tinder season)
awaiting the waters of March

*

the evening sky spreads out
like a mat
for a sun about to sleep
distant trees wave orange hands
to a homing prince.

*

broadfaced like a Kabuki mask
the westering sun
dips a bloodshot eye
in the eloquent eye
of an evening lake

*

a desperate match
stabs the night
in the gloomy alleys
of NEPA's* darkdom
the distance glows
with sparks of amber blood.

*

a careless match, a harmattan rage
our farms are tinder
for a dispossessing flame;
a criminal torch, an incendiary plot
a blaze conceals the trails
of looters of state.

*National Electric Power Authority

Our Earth Will Not Die

(To a solemn, almost elegiac tune)

Lynched
    the lakes
Slaughtered
    the seas
Mauled
    the mountains

But our earth will not die

Here
  there
    everywhere
a lake is killed by the arsenic urine
from the bladder of profit factories
a poisoned stream staggers down the hills
coughing chaos in the sickly sea
the wailing whale, belly up like a frying fish,
crests the chilling swansong of parting waters.

But our earth will not die.

Who lynched the lakes. Who?
Who slaughtered the seas. Who?
Whoever mauled the mountains. Whoever?

Our earth will not die

And the rain
the rain falls, acid, on balding forests
their branches amputated by the septic daggers
of tainted clouds

Weeping willows drip mercury tears
in the eye of sobbing terrains
a nuclear sun rises like a funeral ball
reducing man and meadow to dust and dirt.

But our earth will not die.

Fishes have died in the waters.   Fishes.
Birds have died in the trees.   Birds.
Rabbits have died in their burrows.   Rabbits.

But our earth will not die

(*Music turns festive, louder*)

Our earth will see again
eyes washed by a new rain
the westering sun will rise again
resplendent like a new coin.
The wind, unwound, will play its tune
trees twittering, grasses dancing;
hillsides will rock with blooming harvests
the plains batting their eyes of grass and grace.
The sea will drink its heart's content
when a jubilant thunder flings open the skygate
and a new rain tumbles down
in drums of joy.
Our earth will see again

this earth, OUR EARTH.

From Moonsongs

III

I must be given words to refashion futures like a healer's hand
                                        Edward Kamau Brathwaite

We called the statue
To a talking feast
Before knowing the chisel
Never left a tongue in its rigid mouth . . .

> From the silence of the seasons
> From the hush which murdered the wind
> With thunder's sword
> We borrow the restless throat of *adoko*.*
> We borrow the permanent query
> Of the parrot's beclamoured beak

From the vowel of the river
From the consonant of striving valleys
We name the moon, we name the sun
We pledge a fluent chatter to the stammering sea

From seasons which pass but never part
I borrow moonbeams to shape the wind.

*The adoko is a bird noted for incessant songs.

V

Frantic as a prentice poet
the young moon unfolds,
a wickless lamp
in the silence of lingering nights

trees preen their tops
walls unplug their ears
and hills advance,
minding every crater
on memory's road

moonrays have flared into song
the ballad sizzles in the chimney
of crooning noses;
stars red up the sky
with echoes of silver breaths

can it smell the echo, can it see the chant
a sky whose ears are sealed
by the wax of waning moons?

can it hear
when syllables thrum angry triggers
and consonants fall from heaven
like a hail of vengeful scorpions?

like a troubador
the moon unfolds her songs
by the dusty roadsides of the sky;
the moon unfolds her songs
nomadic like a restless truth

XVIII

The moon is an exile
in the territory of the sky
with a fugitive baggage

ex
    patri
        ated

by hostile fumes
and unrepentant poisons
of foreign factories

The moon flees the sea
with a mercury tear
in each eye:
the whales bemoan their flanks;
sands cannot manage
their pestilence of crabs

And from brimming banks
pampered barons telescope moonface
with glitters of looted quarries,
gaping monarchs tickle moonmaidens
with their noisy crowns
and pliant hacks ply skyroute
with scrolls of our ravished history . . .

Oh cycle of fugitive triumphs;
night peddles frantic eggs with missing yolk:
but dawn tends the bloom of breathing winds.

XIX

A madding moon
has sold the stars
sold the rocks
there is a bickering banter

in the budget of the sky.
The moon plundered the gold
drained the diamonds
and bartered its silvery ore

to the merchants of night
whose claws are cold
whose teeth are crowded tusks
of the ivory of our dreams

The moon has felled the forests
laundered the lakes
harassed the hills:
a yellowing chill stalks

the steps of lunar magnates.
The moon borrows a bullion from Mars
pawns hapless moonchildren to Jupiter;
and when skysages challenge

the dimness of the deeds
the moon pleads its sword,
pleads the bayonet tongue
of its eager guns

Now the moon has crowned our silence
gripped our songs
laid a frenzied ambush
for the syllable of our sooth

A madding moon
has sold the stars . . .
and when a wounded thunder
seeks the sanctity of the skies

Ah! the moon, the moon
will be one rotting pumpkin
in the fringes
of a smoking dawn.

Goree

March, 1989

I

The sun plants a foot in the pasture
Of the sea, reaps one brave shimmer
In the acreage of a ravishing noon;
The Sahel's sizzling glitter enthralls the palms
Beyond the fat-bottomed dialect of the baobab
Where egrets trade roosts with capering crows
And History's large-toed footprints sculpt
Salty tonalities on the open memory
Of Senegal's enchanting depths

At one with sea-birds, clinically white,
Taxiing down the blue, blue tarmac
Of its glassy face, the sea laughs
Through its teeth of feathers,
Fans its liquid cheeks with
A wardrobe of sails,
Before pawing the heat's tropical biceps
With the rapid fancy of flying waters

Noon
And sand-scarred shells explode
Like pods yielding, finally,
To the seven-tongued thunder
Of rainless seasons

      And the Atlantic pounds the shores
      A misty mob of foaming sharks

2

Our ferry furrows through the water,
A rumbling hippopotamus with
A traffic of rainbow laughters;
Pensters, poets, pilgrims, of dappled heels;
The gun this time is a smoking pen,
The cannon only a famous name
For a camera which adores its lens

      And the Atlantic pounds the shores
      A misty mob of foaming sharks

3

We trace the way of the gun
    our wake a liquid memory of billowing tracks

We trace the way of the gun
    our paddles so redolent with orchestrated silence

We trace the way of the gun
    through broken shoals and simmering depths

We trace the way of the gun
    through sad cannon of spent battles

We trace the way of the gun
　　through whip-arched colonnades of bleeding baobabs

We trace the way of the gun
　　through shifty sands and the sombre lyric of peated bones

　　　　And the Atlantic pounds the shores
　　　　A misty mob of foaming sharks

4

Gales, gulls　　　　　　　Shoals, shells
a choir of winds　　　　　　a wilderness of shrieks

Wrists, (r)ankles　　　　　Skulls, silences
a fiesta of chains　　　　　a parliament of sands

　　　　Masters, monsters
　　　　a connonade of edicts

　　　　And the Atlantic pounds the shores
　　　　A misty mob of foaming sharks

5

Castle. Slave castle:
Stone slabs, concrete stairs,
Thick like a plague, deaf like
An orphanning dome;
The cannibal creak of wooden floors
Up, up, where windows open to an endless sea
And echoing orders return, with in-salts
Of flaying accents.

Castle. Slave castle
Eaves of ponderous iron,
Doors on nerveless hinges;
The sea is one limitless moat
Of bristling waters,
The bridge one leaden law in Europe's capacious mouth

    And the Atlantic pounds the shores
    A misty mob of foaming sharks

6

The sea's barbed breeze,
The wounded stammer of receding waves
The lingering thud of syncopated twilights
Rafts which log the distance like floating shadows
Before soaring skywards, a fleet of shrieking crows
Sails fluttering the mist like tattered scarves
Prows bubbling down the waves like sniffing snouts
Belted helmsmen, the drunken genius of cannibal compass

Up, up, here where windows open to an endless sea,
An armada of questions lays siege, still,
At the gate of History's tongue

    And the Atlantic pounds the shores
    A misty mob of foaming sharks

7

Hell. Descent into hell
Into the sticky blackness of hell's pitdom
Fleshports.
Bodies limb to limb with the sweaty glue
Of de-oxygenated dungeons;
The wingless odour of trampled shit,
Nails lengthening into scorpions,
   The whip's pornographic map
   In the atlas of stubborn shoulders,
Manacled calvary on the creed of wailing stones
Damp. Dog-nose damp

Lampless leaps. Bottled rage
Dusty deaths. Rimes in rust.
Feverish squadron of pampered mosquitoes
Damp. Dog-nose damp.

Stolen suns. Stolen stars.
The sky is a pebble in the leopard's eye,
Earth penny-wide under the fettered feet,
And moments tortured by the free laughter
Of teasing waves
Damp. Dog-nose damp

     And the Atlantic pounds the shores
     A misty mob of foaming sharks

8

Memories
Of twilight torches
And nights of flaming cannon
Of blind, blind spears and palaces of cannibal clowns
Of misty mirrors and perfidies of joyless toys

And the gin, the djinni, which routed royal wit,
The millenial belch of flesh feasts,
Of the long manacled trek towards the sea
            towards the sea towards the sea towards . . .

Memories
Of the monkey who mangled the mongoose
For the pleasure of the waiting leopard

            And the Atlantic pounds the shores
            A misty mob of foaming sharks

9

The night without its moon
                without its moon
                without its moon
The day with--out its sun

The hashish of Harlem
Brixton's battered brick
Soweto's narrow chambers
In the castle of our skin

Memories
Of the new dealers:
Their long, long claws, the wildness of their teeth,
Trading old scars for new wounds,
Bankers and *kernbas*, mortgagers and *gamorgers**,
Fresh-finned sharks in the Atlantic of our new peonage

Memories
For how can the hill so rapidly forget
The fragrance of its echo?

> And the Atlantic pounds the shores
> A misty mob of foaming sharks

10

Goree. Gory. Go-awry.
The birds which sing here borrow a note from Elmina,
Their nest bears a straw from the bleeding palms
Of Badagry, of Bagamoyo;
A strife-spun quilt, the wardrobes of our History,
A strife-spun quilt which threads the course
Of absent rainbows.

> And the Atlantic pounds the shores
> A misty mob of foaming sharks

*anagrams: formed for their sound effects

Lupenga Mphande

Why the old woman limps

Do you know why the old woman sings?
She is sixty years old with six grandchildren to look after
While her sons and their wives are gone south to dig gold.
Each day she milks the goat, sells the milk to buy soap,
Feeds and washes the children, and tethers the goat.
In the evening she tells all stories of old at the fireside:
I know why the old woman sings.

Do you know when the old woman sleeps?
She rests with the dark, at night she thinks of
Tomorrow: she's to feed the children and graze the goat.
She's to weed the garden, water the seedling beans,
The thatch has to be mended, the barnyard cleared.
Maize pounded, chaff winnowed, millet ground, fire lit . . .
I do not know when the old woman sleeps.

Do you know why the old woman limps?
She goes to fetch water in the morning
        and the well is five miles away,
Goes to fetch firewood with her axe
        and the forest is five miles the other way,
Goes to the fields to look for pumpkin leaves
        leaving the goat tethered to the well tree
And hurries home to the children to cook:
I know why the old woman limps.

the wood-cutter

When I arrived some clansmen had already come,
Their misty coughs sand muffled whispers permeating
The quiet of the valley, punctuating songs of bulbuls.
This is the season of shift cultivation, said one,
These deciduous trees have to be cut and set alight
Before they shed, and let the humus nurture the millet.
I shivered, waiting for the sun to light up the task;

Nothing could have pleased Yada more: his axe unslung
He leapt up the large tree that flanked the anthill
Looping from branch to branch sizing up the boughs,
His axe flashing in the sun's rays as it swung
And ate into ebony rind, the breeze whizzling,
Throwing Yada's clothes in waves of wrestling
Cruciform shadows on the foliage;

Glistening in morning sun, he whistled out sweat
Streaming down his face, breathing in quick thuds
As he chopped branches one by one, until the last
Crashed into the undergrowth releasing a great wind.
Cloyed by the waft of crushed aloes flowering late,
I wondered which side a severed tree trunk falls
And imagined a weatherman trapped by a storm unforecast.

Tanure Ojaide

When tomorrow is too long

And if a juggler ever arrives in town
with an eagle in a glittering cage,
beware of gifts and numbers.
Beware of the season, beware
of twilight and worse . . .

His closed fist presses
a honeyed cake into an ashen loaf.
With his gap-toothed shine for a wand
he throws out one thing
with one hand
and with the same five
takes in more than seven.
I have been a victim of inflation.

And he says
we are born to be beneficiaries
or victims-- 'you cannot be head
and tail; one or the other.'
His attendants, poster-pasters,
frolic in the loot of a flood;
the rest of the world
live in a drought of denials!

If there's ever a juggler in town
with an eagle in a glittering cage,
shun all the trappings of democracy,
do not allow him perform;
he is bound to be the beneficiary
of all accounts
and you the victim
of that gap-toothed shine of a wand.
Do to him what you'll do
to a cobra in your doorstep;
let tomorrow be too long.

Ward 6

Chekhov, my country is Ward 6.
Nikita, a hound who can cheat a carcass,
takes care of the inmates;
Dr Ragin can't order a clean-up
and, by the way, has given up visits--
he takes beer when Darya gives him,
receives his postmaster friend
and also Khobotov, the tortoise who wants
his position (the menace of high office).

Pain ravages the land,
contorts the mind to tears--
the whip reviles justice,
hunger dismisses fair play,
and the poor know it best.
It always hurts at the bottom
and Dr Ragin's philosophy is meant
for the likes of the London Club,
not for the South or the fourth world.

Gromov, if he were my compatriot,
would laugh at the doctor's corpse
though too late for the dead to say
yes, the trap is everywhere;
suffering has become a birthright
and pain kills, a tyrant and a disease.
There's no coming to terms with the rule.

Here too, Chekhov,
in the long night of miscarriages
we await dawn, a new birth
when killing the damned rotter isn't enough
but drowning him in the pit-latrine
for great grandchildren to live in another country,
free of excoriating pain, free of this disease.

What they said . . .

They called her a cat
because she would not leave him alone.
He knew that she cared--
they saw her from their gossip corners
and he from her own bosom.

They said time would consume them
as they spent themselves.
Rather it fortified them
to withstand waves of assault.
They said time would satiate them
and turn them from one another.
Rather it whetted them
with hungrier appetites for each other.
They said time would separate them
by diminishing their grip on one another.
Rather it housed them under one roof.
They said the earth would soil them
and make them part ways.
Rather it made them a comfortable bed.
They said life would change them
and make them strangers to themselves.
Rather it made them constant--
human, in and out.

(April, 11, 1987)

Launching Our Community Development Fund

It was announced in the *Daily Times*, the *New Nigerian*,
the television, radio, and other acclaimed megaphones.
Today we launch our Community Development Fund
to complete the project the Government abandoned from start
for lack of funds; the Treasury was looted overnight
by those elected to generate national wealth.
Dancers are back again from their holes, gyrating
in front of the Chairman and the Chief Launcher, millionaires.
The booths are painted bright in national colours.
In those days as dancers twisted themselves out of breath
to the applause of the Governor and his vast entourage,
we laid foundation stones with party blocks that dissolved
with the return of the Honourable Guest to the capital –
the budget allocation went with the civic reception.
There was no attempt to build what would outlive the builders,
and this disregard for afterlife was unfortunate for us
Christians and Muslims; heaven could not be gained here.
Today, as before, there are dancers to excite the chiefs
to pledge millions of naira to build their egos.
Always before new lords that rise with the fall of old patrons,
the dancers live eternally digging the ground that swallows
the Very Impotent Personalities. And after this launching,
the proceedings, the names of donors, will be announced
in the *Daily Times*, the *New Nigerian* and other acclaimed
megaphones.

Musaemura Zimunya

Arrivants

They came back home from bush-haunts
and refugee camps the living and the dead;
they flew back from misery's northern coldness
and humiliation's faithful missionaries abroad
to colours, bunting, pennants and earthborn songs
that awoke History and tradition with a bang-bang.

Came to Hope-dawns and democracy with strings attached
and so we were reconciled to white faces
whose pride and heads had watered UDI and racism –
aren't they keen to teach us compassion!

The year sped on caterpillar wheels as a result
but our ninety-year old patience seemed to have endless reach
so we could still listen to the critics of our monthly
emigration statistics without wishing for another Ben-Bella.

Then, also, Bulawayo was a place of killing again
to remind us that our peace was a hasty marriage
where we had no training camps for the new order –
to say that the power of peace must in the new age
reside in hearts of Ndebele and Shona, not in gun-barrels.

Yet when quiet returned in the area of madness
Chaminuka's words came torrenting and torrenting
and seriously we wondered who would stop this Rain,
or dare we murder another *mhondoro**?

Or dare we have more petals of blood simply
because someone's whim pleads for more petals of blood
tomorrow and tomorrow when most want life and rest?
We, indeed, are arrivants with blister-feet and broken bones
that will learn the end of one journey
begins another.

*mhondoro is Shona for spirit-medium.

Kisimiso

The family were gathered
the eldest son from Bulawayo
boastful of his experiences in the city of knives and crooks;
one son from Harare,
a fish-pocket who can slang everyone
into ignorance with the stupefying s'kuz'apo* tongue
(the family believe he is the chief mechanic at Lever Brothers!);
a sister, latest to arrive, from Gutu
blue-painted eye-lids, false eye-lashes, red lips
bangles gritting in her hands
with a European hair-wig above an Ambi-proof face
she covers her thighs with a towel when she sits
(as for her the family will always believe she is a dressmaker
        in Fort Victoria);
the rest of the family, mum and dad, are happy to
        admire the latest from town.

Kisimiso means feasting
dozens of bread loaves, drums of tea, mountains of *sadza*
rock-size pieces of meat of the he-goat
in lakes of thousand-eyed soup
and, of course, large pots of fizzing frothy beer.
Nothing about the print themes of good will and peace
of course good will was always here;
and old man well-known to me lost half his hair
while pulling a tourist out of a blazing car's wreckage – in
June,
six months before last Christmas.

A child without clothes sat nodding with sleep
his belly as big as a *muchongoyo*† drum:
buzzing flies were fighting, spinning and tumbling
into the smelling parting between his buttocks,
Kutu the scraggy dog was retching in front of him;
they ultimately gave the mother water that
had washed the madman's beard
because she could no longer leave the bush
or close her oozing behind
and brother *s'kuz'apo*
filled the boys' hut with urine and vomit
and a powerful smell of beer gone stale.

The next day
they talked of the greatest Kisimiso
for many years.

---

*s'kuz'apo is urban slang for 'excuse-me there'.
†muchongoyo is Shona for a vibrant traditional dance.

Frank Chipasula

A Love Poem for my Country

for James

I have nothing to give you, but my anger
And the filaments of my hatred reach across the border.
You, you have sold many and me to exile.
Now shorn of precious minds, you rely only on
What hands can grow to build your crumbling image.

Your streets are littered with handcuffed men
And the drums are thuds of the warden's spiked boots.
You wriggle with agony as the terrible twins, law and order,
Call out the tune through the thick tunnel of barbed wire.

Here, week after week, the walls dissolve and are slim,
The mist is clearing and we see you naked like
A body that is straining to find itself but cannot
And our hearts are thumping with pulses of desire or fear
And our dreams are charred chapters of your history.

My country, remember I neither blinked nor went to sleep
My country, I never let your life slide downhill
And passively watched you, like a recklessly-driven car,
Hurrying to your crash while the driver leapt out.

The days have lost their song and salt.
We feel bored without our free laughter and voice.
Every day thinking the same and discarding our hopes.
Your days are loud with clanking cuffs
On men's arms as they are led away to decay.

I know a day will come and wash away my pain
And I will emerge from the night breaking into song
Like the sun, blowing out these evil stars.

Ritual Girl

There is a girl dragging heavy
foot-chains, drained of her dance;
The razor sharp barbed wire
cuts deep into her bound wrists.

We nicknamed her butterfly,
lusty brown skin, dark fertile land;
painted lips like a fresh sore,
scorched hair straight like bamboos,

she could pass for a roadside bar whore
as she fainted under her ninth man
in a row, her dance ebbing slowly:

Pound me as you dehusk your maize
Wash me like you wash your millet
Thrash me like you strip your rice
Till I am burning, spent and pure.

That was in college, many moons ago, yet
my mind hugs the clear-cut images
of her dreamy eyes like lunar lakes
we worshipped, sought in reverence;

frail lecherous flesh, sensuous dimples,
insatiate grave, every sailor's port
of call where seagulls led us to rest
where we searched for cool clear water.

The snake-skinned banjo wailed for her
plaintively, the tea-chest bass groaned for her.
We loved her as every exile loves the *patrie*;
Now our laments flow through every poem.

The lips of the singers are heavy
with her suitors' names fed to the lions;
in the dark dungeons her lovers languish
as she drags the heavy foot-irons painfully.

Talking of Sharp Things

for Jack Mapanje and Lupenga Mphande

I think of the razor-sharp knife
slicing through the sweetness
of a ripe mango, thoroughly ravaging
the layers of life's plentitude, its juice
running over as barbed wire digs
into bonded arms: who relishes the flesh
What thirst does this blood quench?
I think of the great sorrows of flesh
Of the country with my face mapped
with bullet-holes, machete and knobkerrie
scarred, bleeding, the arrow quivering
in its torn heart that still dances;
a heart that has vowed to sing always
Bleeding, how red the river waters,
Bleeding into the water-wells
where we all suckle at the distended breast.
My mirror shifts a little yet leaves its
edge which cuts my clear image on my land,
in the lines my inherited sweat collects.
We patch up the land with our gaping wounds;
I think of the adze that cuts a man out of wood,
Of spears cutting down a life built of labour.

I talk of pain as sharp as a hunter's dagger
Though it does not bring respite to exile.
Unseen as it is, I still talk of pain
As if it were the sharp claws of the flag cock.
I think of thorns and those other thorns
A crown full of thorns and a king who is dying
of indulgence, and a rough tree that holds him;
And of the hands that have been torn

And the hands drained of all tenderness, hands
that cannot hug or fondle without throttling
And of the mouth that will never sing again
Without a splinter of rail threatening it
Without the edge of a *phanga* guarding it
I think of other thorns lodged in the throats –
Now I talk of that which is double-pointed
And spares no one, even those who do not talk
I speak of them too and whatever spear got them,
And of Narcissus and sadist goading and laughing
His ribs split by a happiness lined with pain.
I must stop and wonder how the armless wind
whips stings pierces tears and escapes uncaught!
And of slogans that are launched like harpoons
And of the many who have perished under them

And of sharp jagged rocks hurled at the enemy
And of all those patriots shouting, 'Stone him!
Stone him!' And the rushing, thrashing until what was
becomes only pulp cast into the rivers
insatiable as the mass graves dotted across the land.
I shall speak of betrayal too and the last supper
in which shrapnel is hidden and served or
the spring mattress with pointed knives in the foam
and of the man who took the woman violently
there and paid for it in his blood;
And of the land that suffers silently like sheep;
Of the strange wedge driven permanently between people
Hallelujah! Of the nails and the heavy hammers
pinning the flesh and its attendant sins to crucifix
and of the death drooping down the rough wood.
And then three cheers for the Party and threefold for
The Leader a snake in three-piece rich rags and a mouth
endowed with incisors and fangs and words that bite
and kill like the sharp tail of the whirlwind dancing

in our country, descending the mountains and gripping
the trees, uprooting them and sweeping the valleys.

I have to talk of this or that, of love perhaps,
and stumble or stammer on that forbidden word
or of a kiss whose fangs completely rip off the lovers' lips;
of massacres and mass axe murders and the sale of blood
to South Africa crossing apartheid's lines, always mysterious
deeds done in the deep nights, Chilobwe or something
And ramble sometimes as chaotic as the world;
I have to talk of Messiahs, their cathedrals and sword-like
spires that rend our pagan hearts as they convert them;
Perhaps of a blind root that burrows instinctively
And attempts desperately to reach the depths of our lives.
Maybe I must talk of the man who carries pain in
                                        himself intimately
like a child that waits to be born, but refuses to die.
But now let me turn to a needle and its invisible thread

and the tattered body of my country that waits to be sewn.

Going Back Patiently

And here we are back
to the point we started from
trying to trace the path we took
but finding only traces and trails of ash
on burned down tarmac highways
showing that we too contributed
to our own destruction
letting it go on
as if it never mattered.

And if we should decide
we shall clear a new one elsewhere
in the depths of the lost primeval forest
which was facelifted and grafted
upon foreign streets for pavement
all glittering with false imitation rubies
we are back to the untimed times
and must dig and patiently too.

Then we scan the footprints of our memory
and imagination for possible clues
But violent winds have mercilessly blown
them out of our boulder-smashed minds
pell-mell into dust clouds
and laughing breezes watch us patiently digging.

Going back patiently
to starting points, eavesdropping
at keyholes to the locked past
we are punished for window-peeping
And we must ask and ask and ask
about the hidden road that Chilembwe took,
sitting at crossroads in dilemma
watching our leaders embrace our enemies;
or starting off again on the blind road.

My Blood Brother

First we locked our fingers, wove them
round each other, and murmured our brother-
hood promises: To protect each other
in time of attack and to love each other as
if from the same womb and share everything equally.

Then, with a razor sharpened with love
You cut your wrist and I mine incised.
I kissed your arm and sucked your blood
And you drank mine, sealing the bond.
We squeezed our blood into the baobab fruit,
stirred it together with the baobab milk
And together, under the mango tree, drank
the concoction, and shared our first fish.

Do you remember, Blood Brother, 1959
and the hailstorm of colonial bullets we braved
through, marching our arms locked tightly together
our hearts, almost fused into one, beating to each
other through the gun-smoke and bursting flames?
Remember, my blood flows through your veins
And your precious blood is mine, I will not
break the invisible knot

Brother, though you came from the mountains
And I from the depths of the lake, sea-weed
in my eyes and the sun on my mouth, and the smell
of fish all over my body, that love that bound
you to me erased all that could differentiate us.
But today the Party has come between us like a wizard
and it is planting the seeds of hatred in our
different paths; you have gathered your mouth
into terrible tucks and sewn it and you know my fear
of silent men: A silent man hides war in his heart.
Today, you point a dagger at my heart, the Party armed you.
Remember the vow we took and remember the blood
That flows through me to you in a continuous path.

Those Rainy Mornings

*for my aunt aGwalanthi, with sweet memories after Robert
Hayden's* Those Winter Sundays

Mondays my aunt awoke with the first cockcrow, in
                                    the orange dawn,
placed the porridge pot on the fire, making it sing to rain taps,
over leaping flames licking its sooty buttocks
and with her tough hoe-broken palms,
broke the rain-wet wood across her knee, feeding the fire.

I'd slither slowly out of the nagging nightmare
of a giant witch to her soft shadow
dancing, swerving, on the rough mud wall
and the crackling firewood and her soft, but husky call

Thinking of the torn sagging umbrella, chalk dust and
                                    this rugged
woman who had embraced responsibility over these children
whose parents had strayed to the copper mines.
How could I see, oh how could I see
The great soft heart beating behind those scrawny ribs.

Because the Wind Remembers

For David
Remembering Mbalame: the film, the bird

The hideous laughter
of your invisible mockingbird
still hangs at the edge
of my sleep, tears through my dreams.
The rock that flattens a brother's chest
letting out that bitter crimson river
flowing incessantly in our land
turns my dreams into nightmares.
The dark wind sobs and hangs its tears
on the night air and the moon
light that burns through it.
Because the wind remembers
Because its thundering sobs are our own;
in it are the howled exclamations
of bursting genitals squeezed
between blunt pincers in dark dungeons
and the huge teeth of the whip
biting into the flesh of our country
This wild breath of the bleeding wind
caught like lace round the emaciated legs
of a village dance drunk on blood
screams as the dawn is plunged into night.
The bird's deep whimper in the dense woods
stabs the lake with a secret lightning.
Ah, there goes again its raw ghostly
laughter like heavy guns thundering.

My Friendly People

The pulse of your revolt stilled,
Smiles stained with blood on your lips;
Where is your violence
Do not deny me that hatred
you pointed like a sword
against the master, ah my friendly
people flashing silly plastic teeth!
Yesterday, only guns could answer your fury:
Today, you smile sickly from postcards.
That morning you shook this land
with your united roar of lions;
tonight you dance your anger into the soil,
your legs drowsily stomping
your fire into the dust.
Happy, yes, happy they call you,
those that stand too far away
to see the streams of your tears.
The sons of men who towered tall
like our palm trees or baobabs,
are they these cowards prostrating before
false lions that flee their shadows?
Those days you tore apart the night
with one voice; today the night covers
your eyes like a thick, rough counterpane.
Is it because you are tired of bleeding
Or that you bled all your blood fighting
violently for the British king?
Show me today one glittering piece of metal
that was not polished with your blood.
Well, it's true, it was not your guns
that you lifted up, aimed and fired.
They lent you their violence like a bitter
wine barrelled in their guns, and once drunk

and reeling and reeking, awakened your own.
True, someone not of your own made a huge bomb
to finish off thousands of other humans –
Your eyes are not as lethal as all that!
But still there was that dormant fire in your
muscle that alien hatred awakened;
I want to borrow that fire to brand love on our land.

Tramp

He trudges the streets of Blantyre
weighed down by his KAR 'medals':
pierced Coca-Cola bottle tops,
funeral bands and decorations, shouting:
Africa for the Africans! before tourists
their cameras clicking incessantly as
he recounts memories of the dark bomb shelters
in the last battle of Tanganyika:
cycling a stationary bicycle tied
to the roof to keep the lamp burning
the boys singing for morale and how
with *phangas*, bayonets and muscle
they 'trounced' the Germans for their masters.

He tramps from bar to bar, sack over shoulder,
gathering half-drunk bottles of Carlsberg beer
and cigarette butts from rich people's ashtrays
for the victory party that he will hold
with the spirits of his slain colleagues
whom he salutes in his solitary minute of silence
remembering Burma and cheap women in eastern brothels,
Zomba and Nyasa camps, cannon and thunder
on the wooded banks of the yellow river.

And when we shower him with *tambala* coins
for a thrill, he smiles, his glassy eyes smarting
and like a khaki robot he drills stiffly
for another war he only knows, fingers
his stars, black stripes, and softly weeps
for a wife violated in absence, his land gone,
the promised compensation he will not see.
We watch him burn into ash like a cigarette
as he talks of blood in the red strip of the banner,
the setting sun casting darkness over his lost land
all so green, all so green, yet gone, going;
And he sulks, murmuring of the blood spilt in the struggle,
of the bullets turned into bees in *Operation Dawn*
human targets melting into lakes and mirages in Mulanje
and the fifty innocents massacred mercilessly at Nkhata Bay.

And when we query him about the contents
of his sticky soiled sack, he answers: 'Promises'
and embraces his silence again.

Friend, Ah You Have Changed!

A river never flows back into its source.

Ah, friend you have changed; neckless,
your smile is so plastic
your cheeks are blown-out balloons
and your once accordion ribs
are now drowned under mountains of fat;
your belly is a river in flood threatening your head,
your woollen three-piece exaggerates the cold.

Prisoner behind high concrete walls
wearing transparent crowns of broken glass,
guarded by sharp-toothed bulldogs
whose barks pierce the spines of passers-by
and spiked gates standing firmly vigilant
as you entertain company with imported spirits
bought with the people's tax money,
discussing your mischiefs, rallies where you fed
your audiences on false promises.

I am still where you left me, strapped ever to my hoe
in the dust, my fingers clutching the discarded rosary
praying for rain to grow enough for the Party,
put Boyi in school and pay the soaring hospital bills
while the priest claims his half for God Almighty
sending the eternal fire raging, through my mind.

Though I am pushed near the edge
of your skyscraping platform to touch your shoe for
                                        salvation
you do not see me, your eyes rivetted on imaginary
enemies whom you vanquish with our chorus strung
                                        together.
The picture men will not notice me buried in this crowd
and the papers will print your shout clearly into news.

Ah friend, how you have changed,
You will never flow back here.

From NIGHTWATCHER, *Nightsong*

I: Dusk

Nightwatcher:
Fast falls the night unfurling its vile veil
Showering its soot into our eyes plunging us into deep darkness
Extinguishing the fiery flame of the spent sun
The sharp shrilling shrieks of the first detainees
Herded into dark catacombs of Mikuyu and Chingwe's hole
Drown in the maenadic frenzy of the ululating chorus bitches
Brandishing party cards, passports to feasting houses
As dust fills the crowing cock's mouth taking it for dawn:
Then death goes hunting through men's huts with long knives.

Nightwatcher:
Carrion birds dig and probe with their erect lethal beaks
Into the Chibuku-beer drenched bodies of the chorus bitches
Hawking genitals, stirring, inflaming their lust for farms, cars,
Houses, plane-rides into a frenzy of butt-wriggling dances
Stirred into the chalice to sweeten the gory sacrificial wine
At the sumptuous midnight banquets for the devil ·
The cantors parrot praise songs and slogans
As the ferocious tame leonine Messiah rides the death chariot
Stirring the coarse dust of dissent with his wicked horse-tail.

Nightwatcher:
These streets are tired and drowsy, sleepless feet drag heavy
                                                    chains,
Lamp-posts weep under the cold dead weight of the crimson
                                                    dew
Condensed out of the flow from the feet pierced by sharp barbs
As they cudgel them through the nets into the House of Seven
                                                    Locks
While the deep nightfall veils the secret murders in its shroud
Muffles the painful wails of the bereaved wives, mothers and
                                                    children,
Knits our brows with beeswax and drugs us into submissive
                                                    stupor
Like bees smoked in our tree-cave hideouts and dark dungeons.

Nightwatcher:
The dwarfed despot descends his lofty ivory throne of polished
                                                                bones
Dips into the bathtub filled with human blood
Splashes frantically for the saving straw, sinks slowly into the
                                                                quagmire
Drunk on the bitter champagne of tears from battered babies
From the chalice of polished human skulls he drinks
The great lion devoid of leonine mercy mauls his own
With the song of the screech owl and the nightjar in his ears.

Nightwatcher:
The same teeth that threatened to rip the enemy now smile
At the same men as their arms gather and embrace him
                                                                intimately
The same hands that wielded home-made guns and poison
                                                                arrows
Tremble as they shake our foe with the tender warmth of our
                                                                milked land
The same feet that ran and chased the master out of our
                                                                country
Now strut on the platforms in the thick boots left by master.
With these they are tearing the mouths of our people, their new
                                                                enemy.

Nightwatcher, fear is dexterously woven like a dredge net
That tightens its dry iron meshes around each hut
Pain-laden voices escape through the cracked doors and
Spread their blood-tinted gossamer all over the slumbering land.
The official claws are squeezing the dissenting throats
Until the vocal cords snap and the windpipes are totally crushed,
The voices muzzled and the reed flutes discarded, their sweet
song stolen.
Fear has chained them to a boulder that hangs dangerously
over them.

Nightwatcher: Authority passes its clenched fist through the
people's minds
Feeling for the sharp edges of divergent thought
Uniting millions of survival champions of the world
Who have to lie to keep alive from the zealous knobkerries
Of the over-patriotic thugs driving our country into brewing
storms.
Nightwatcher, ten thousand citizens enmeshed in barbed-wire
nets!
Abroad our ambassadors rant and boast about our peace and
calm
While at home we dance on fire and bruise our backs on
thorns:
Fawners crawl, prostrate themselves before the despot,
Lick his boots, polish his ass with their long tongues
Scramble for fallen crumbs under perpetual banquet tables
Praising our chief executioners brandishing gory daggers.

Manifesto On Ars Poetica

My poetry is exacting a confession
from me: I will not keep the truth
from my song and the heartstringed instrument;
The voice undressed by the bees,
I will not bar the voice undressed by the bees
from entering the gourd of my bow-harp.
I will not wash the blood off the image
I will let it flow from the gullet
slit by the assassin's dagger through
the run-on line until it rages in the verbs of terror;
And I will distil life into the horrible adjectives;
I will not clean the poem to impress the tyrant
I will not bend my verses into the bow of a praise song.
I will put the symbols of murder hidden in high offices
in the center of my crude lines of accusations.
I will undress our raped land and expose her wounds.
I will pierce the silence around our land with sharp metaphors
And I will point the light of my poems into the dark
nooks where our people are pounded to pulp.
I will not coat my words in lumps of sugar
I will serve them to our people with the bitter quinine:
I will not keep the truth from my heartstringed guitar;
I will thread the voice from the broken lips
through my volatile verbs that burn the lies.
I will ask only that the poem watch the world closely;
I will ask only that the image put a lamp on the dark
ceiling in the dark sky of my land and light the dirt.
Today, my poetry has exacted a confession from me.

Molara Ogundipe-Leslie

song at the african middle class

For agostinho neto

we charge through the skies of disillusion,
seeking the widening of eyes, we gaze at chaos,
speak to deadened hearts and ears stopped with
commerce. We drift around our region of clowns,
walking on air as dreams fly behind our eyes.
we forage among broken bodies, fractured minds
to find just ways retraced and new like beaten cloth.

and if they come again
will they come again?
and if they come again
will they dance this time?
will the new *egungun* dance once more
resplendent in rich-glassed cloth?
will they be of their people's needs,
rise to those needs, settle whirling rifts
salve, O, festering hearts?
will they say when they come
O my people, O my people, how to love you delicately?

On Reading an Archaeological Article –

on Nefertiti's Reign and Ancient Egyptian Society (Sunday,
New York Times, 9th January 1971).

They would say that she of the neck like a duiker's
Whose breasts are the hills of Egypt
Who weeps the Nile from her eyes of antimony
Is but another Cosmopolitan housewife
Smart enough to walk ten paces behind her Mr. Doe.

O Akhanaton . . . !

How long shall we speak to them
Of the goldness of mother, of difference without bane
How long shall we say another world lives
Not spinned on the axis of maleness
But rounded and wholed, charting through
Its many runnels its justice distributive?

O Nefertiti . . .

Odia Ofeimun

Prologue . . .

I have come down
to tell my story
by the same fireside
around which
my people are gathered

I have come home
to feel for ears and hearts and hands
to rise with me
when I say the words
of my mouth

And I must tell my story
to nudge and awaken them
that asleep
among my people.

How Can I Sing

I cannot blind myself
to putrefying carcases in the market place
pulling giant vultures
from the sky

Nor to these flywhisks:
how can I escape these mind-ripping scorpion-tails
deployed in the dark
with ignominious licence
by those who should buttress faith
in living, faith in lamplights?

And how can I sing
when they stuff cobwebs in my mouth
spit the rheum of their blank sense
of direction in my eyes
– who will open the portals of
my hope in this desultory walk?

Yet I cannot blunt my feelers
to cheapen my ingrained sorrow
I cannot refuse to drink from
the gourd you hold to my lips

A garland of subversive litanies
should answer these morbid landscapes
my land, my woman

Let Them Choose Paths

They choose paths
who think there are paths to choose
They make banners and float
our next republic.

They scour the garbage
of folklore
for the piece of silver
hidden by the wily tortoise.

They seek life
who cower at growths of lianas and creepers,
They run from the tangled stems
in search of stripped wisdom.

Pathfinders, all
they do not dare to know,
the thrill of building roads anew
too soft, too spiritless to stand
the course of sweat
down the smalls of their backs

Let them choose paths
who think there are paths to choose
We, we must grow new eyes
to see the asphalt in the chaste forest.

The Poet Lied

I

He wanted to rise up to the moment
to be on the side of those
who became relevant,
those whose voices spelled out balanced concern
when his country was dipped like a dishrag
in the blood of her own children.
He meant to escape the acute fever
the immoderacy of the rabble
the learned folly of his drunk ex-comrades
who strutted about in prison dungeons
in malarial forests, refugee camps
and in foreign lands
married to war-hoops of one kind
or another.

Not that he hated war-hoops:
he knew how to shock silence
once falsehood became the region of convenience,
he knew how to take sides,
putting salt in ready stew-pots
to gratify the patricians of war.

He asked this much:
to be left alone
with his blank sheets on his lap
in some dug-out damp corner
with a view of the streets and the battlefields
watching the throng of calloused lives,
the many many lives stung by living.
He would put them into his fables
sandwich them between his lions and eagles,
between his elephants and crocodiles

Sometimes if he felt like it
he would come away from his corner
to take a closer look at things
fishermen in their canoes, hounded by tides,
swimmers drowning, hounded by tides
And he would take snapshots-
no need to caption them-
he would not mind at all
if he was called the poet of snapshots,
a quack of visions, a quack of visions.

II

He was not a guerrilla fighter,
he sniffed about, disdaining
those who hatched themselves out
of their ivory bunkers
to strike some blow
for the many helpless of the earth.

For him as for the many handy serfs
to whose lot it fell
to whitewash the public idols
with termite-eaten insides,
there was no place for raised fingers
even when human adders
gobbled the peace of the market place,
even when famine snaked through
his neighbours' homesteads
he saw no need for raised fingers.

He wanted to be left alone
to spin his shallow legends, his shy songs
out of the dastardised living of his kind
out of the spectacle of aged mothers
defiled by maniacs
under the noses of their first-born.

He asked this much; to be left alone
to celebrate what his skin was too thick
to absorb. And for this
this and nothing else
he would write his name on the sands
and dare storms to blot it out.

III

Against the rash of public sins
necklacing the national psyche like prize medals,
the little deaths which besieged
the life of every man woman and child
spawned by political pimps and truth benders,
he shut the judas-eye of his camera.
Where he cared, he ladled gruel,
cold tasteless soup dumplings into the jaws
of a ghosted anguished world.
When he wrote, he pasted weather reports
colourless, snippety, thumps of items
about friends who died, comrades slain
in the frenzied billows of civil strife.

The memory of his once-loved ones
he brushed away with shrewd words,
words without *feel* or *let-go*
neuters debasing the quality of the pain
the sadness and the blot
to which events sentenced the crying need
of his fellow countrymen for new visions.

IV

Shunning the warm-blooded stance
of the town-crier
whose gong deigned to rouse
the slumbering populace to face
their own, their very own experiences,
he lacked, even where he tried to own,
the legend-spinner's deference
for the communal fireplace

For his songs aspired to knead concern
by deadening the roots the navel that binds
the living to their kind and native land
For his voice was cold, sandpaperish,
farming no honesty,
Weeping to measured effects, in false fits
he laminated the wind with cat-calls
where there ought to be thunder.

Where his heart should burst
his words were merely correct and sane,
the envy of the gazette-compilers
lacking the energy, the human inflexion to exhume
from their shallow makeshift graves
the memory of those lost
in paths of rain and ruin

And because he tried to change
the exuberant colours of life
into sallow marks, relieving death
of its hurt, its significance,
the poet lied, he lied hard.

A Naming Day

Festive draperies override the claims of
bread and fresh air in this house

Gaudy buntings take breath away
from the newborn muffled in damask

in lace, in nameless riots of colours
Mothers redress the loss of breast-milk

(so indecent to breast-feed children
now that mothers have turned mummies)

Sorcerers of the supermarket conjuring
toys to people the lonesome hours
of unsung nurseries

Mothers have turned mummies
and growing up means to grind and wallow
in adult games of self-deceit
before the antimony of truth has time
to lay its fingers on the little heads

A Handle for the Flutist

You have heard it said before
that poetry makes no water jump
blows not the wind it divines
builds no pyramids nor does it
repair bridges or start anything afresh.

Yet in the common tongue of those
who love to feel the terror of survival
the survival of mouth as mouth alone
the worshipped word is enough
to expiate crimes and to lay honour
upon whom the pleaded grace of song has fallen.

So to save culture, they save a little risk
for those who obey no laws of gravity
outsiders to pain for whom murder will pass
no moral handle to the flutist
they fly only where the executives
would never want to tamper. Where?
The described becomes the prescribed
You have heard it said before.

So while they celebrate themselves
for holy ineffectuality
and seek the freedom of the ostrich
to bury their heads in the sands
let us praise those who will banish poets
from the People's Republic.

Let us praise them who know
what pagan fire can come
from waterfalls denied the lie of valleys
those who have seen gods crumble to their knees
questioned by simple images
so let us praise those who will track down
folksongs with police dogs
They will not live with poets
in the People's Republic.

Beyond Fear

For five journalists who cared

I

The fact that we survive it compels us
to do something about it: the hungerbash
hidden by the syrupy communiques
of the idols of warfare, trade, and 'tricknology'
The fact that we survive
the beleaguered slumscapes
the sweltering, tattered villages,
dragoons of biocide
afester with rancid commerce,
the fact that we survive it
compels us to do something about it,
to scoff and wag our loaded fingers
at the zanny cowboys on heat
heaping salted invectives and trash-talks
at the daring ones who go at dusk
away from the refuge of air-conditioned nightmares

the daring ones who go in mufti
into fevered forests to embrace
the guerrillas of the poisoned swamps

The fact that we survive it
compels us to do something about it
to damn the suavity of yellow robots
who displace the mangled corpses of
men, women and children in Salvador
as in our own backwoods at Bakalori
with media headbutts
to save the world for dollar bills
That fact that we survive it
compels us to do something about it
something about the tall insults of promises
which wipe the sky clean of rainclouds
to create false seasons of drought
in people's minds, in hope-drenched wishes

*

The fact that we survive and can stand
before the pillars of the republic
in clean cocktail coveralls, clinking small-talk
in ever renewed, freshly laundered ideologies
as ancient as peace and prosperity
that fact that we survive
the anomic respectabilities compels us
to nod in empathy when a whole man dies
trying to raise the meaning of joy
to lips that have known only curses
and the vengeful taste of flaming knives.

II

They were not mere hunters for scoops
bitten by the dog-flea of the next-day's headline
The yellow dross in which they drown
who fire and forget themselves
as they fire and forget their kind
in lilting drapes and beatific scapes
made from sacked villages and burnt harvests

They were not mere hunters for scoops
sniffing the foddermash of hounded humanity
in mass graves. They held their hearts
eternal tabloid for the wretched serfs
who have no names in the street
those whose voices are not carried by the wind
because of those whose voices carry the wind.

They were not mere hunters for scoops
In a world turned schizoid by the dicta
of death-worship in paper-money
They pushed the moral handle beyond profit
beyond the arrogance of normless dictators
marketeers of spilt milk, spilt hope, spilt minds
They pushed the moral handle beyond fear.

They were not mere hunters for scoops
quarrying for arty banners in the bloody scare
of maimed careers, maimed lives and cold deaths.
Happy to be seduced by the joy of being human
human and alive they gripped the bitter tale
of other lives within their own. They went
to God as recklessly as only truth can go

They would not romp after the dead
like crocodiles in pilate's lake of tears.

Judgement Day

They will tumble down from rooftops
treetops and hilltops
where they once glowed with the bravura of gods
Their bloated robes smudged by public sins
will billow in the winds as they squirm and gutter
rocking to unbelief the sheep, the touts and clowns
who bleated 'Amen' to their every whip and lash.
They will tumble down
From their towers of illusions,
they will tumble down as they awaken
to the speed of thunderbolts, nemetic music
Their ears, deal to hometruths
will flap in their bullfrog run
amidst the leer and contempt
aimed by the menials
yesterday's carriers of gongs and talking drums
who spread hossana-green palmfronds
halleluyah palmfronds
for their motorcades

They will fall from the dais
dazed by hammerblows
shunned by the neon-lights that once called them,
the feverish handclaps which saw them through,
from whoredoms to whirldoms of insentiate grogginess
They will fall from the dais
bald lives, vultures with clipped wings
They will fall to be received by the sizzling spittle
the aimed rejection, our collective spite
And if they still outwit
the contrition that is theirs
through overdrafts from their long-filliped sin
And if they still outwit the shame that is theirs

in the pride-tall sins that have swamped us all
they cannot escape the healing floods
the legations of looming storms that will break
storms that will stick their hearts to the roofs
    of their mouths
making of them cheap rodents in the blitz
that must weed and sweep the streets
sweeping away the banana skins
that have slimed and could slime
the path of those who would rather throw
than be thrown by the ghomids of public sins.

Catherine Obianuju Acholonu

Other forms of slaughter

there were other forms
of slaughter
you know

when hands of sandpaper
jarr at tender tendons
of daughter drums

there were other forms
of slaughter

when rods of aggression
rip through sealed valves
of flutes of reed

when innocent virgins
basking in the sun
suddenly wake up to
greedy eyes
lecherous tongues
and devouring breath

and gathering their cloths
about them clamber
hurriedly
up the cliff

but heavy boots
are at their heels
heaving chests pin
them down
then greedy hands
rummaging

tear open
the frills of their
delicate legend
unfolding a lustful era
of anarchic bestiality

yeah!
these were other forms of slaughter

Nigeria in the year 1999

today the sixth of june
in the year of our lord
nineteen hundred and ninety nine
a child was born at 6 p.m.

weight – three stones
height – three feet
colour – whitish black

mother died of exhaustion
and father took off on a feat of fear
and what is this bunch of bloody rubbish
has the child been shitting in the womb?
no that is the placenta
I suppose
the what?
is it a cuckoo's nest?
here pieces of broken razor
MADE IN ENGLAND
there heaps of cigarette butts
but no, nothing as mild as that
this is plain harsh 'goof'*

and these reels and reels of tape?
just wait a minute
what has this adult-infant been up to?
provided its own everything
even its own rock'n roll
right from the tomb?
no, womb?

*marijuana

our little man didn't have to yell out his first sound
just switched on his micro-cassette
and bob marley came blaring out

    r-a-st-a f-ar-i-a
    e-x-o-d-u-s

child of the devil has got it all worked out
how to enjoy life in nigeria
then still dripping of blood
infant child says his first words:

here is my pamphlet of 'Life Made Simple'

    chapter one   – how to run without walking

    chapter two   – education made simple
                expo* 2000

    chapter three – how to make billions without
                sweat
                the secret of ten percent

    chapter four – rig yourself into life-presidency

surely our little man
is most highly equipped
for life in nigerian fashion

*examination malpractice (slang)

Chenjerai Hove

Red Hills of Home

Father grew up here
tuning his heart
to the sound of the owl from the moist green hills,
beyond, the eagle swam in the air
while mother-ant dragged
an unknown victim to a known hole
printed on the familiar unreceding earth.

I grew up here,
father died underground seven rainless seasons ago
and the burial news
was all we had to bury.
Now the featherless eagle, like roast meat,
recites the misery of the dusty sky.
Mother-ant never surfaces
for father is enough meat, underground.
The green hills of home died,
Red hills cut the sky
and the nearby sooty homes of peasants
live under the teeth of the roaring bulldozer.
Yesterday sabhuku Manyonga had the push
of muscular hands on his chest
and now lives in drunken exile.

Red hills have come
with wounds whose pus
suffocates the peasant.
The peasant's baby sleeps
knowing only thin dreams of moonlight joy.

Dying too are the songs
of the seasons that father once sang
Red hills and the smoke of man-made thunder
plunder the land under contract.

If father rose from the dead
he would surely not know
the very ant-hill embracing his blood
buried with the umbilical cord.
Here, on this bit of ground
earth once lay pregnant
but now
the sacred hill bleeds
robbed even of her decent name,
her holy cows are milked
by hunger-laden hands
whose mouths eat man
gulped down by this eerie giant's throat
sitting where once you flowed
with calm holy water.

Red hills and the smell of exile;
Chipo died this morning
no more burial song ripped the air
nor do we feel safe to bury her
knowing tomorrow a bulldozer comes
to scatter these malnourished bones.

Red hills, and the smell of exile
Exile breathing over our shoulder
in a race that already looks desperate.
Red hills, and the pulse of exile
telling us this is home no more.

You Will Forget

If you stay in comfort too long
you will not know
the weight of a water pot
on the bald head of the village woman

You will forget
the weight of three bundles of thatch grass
on the sinewy neck of the woman
whose baby cries on her back
for a blade of grass in its eyes

Sure, if you stay in comfort too long
you will not know the pain
of child birth without a nurse in white

You will forget
the thirst, the cracked dusty lips
of the woman in the valley
on her way to the headman who isn't there

You will forget
the pouring pain of a thorn prick
with a load on the head.
If you stay in comfort too long

You will forget
the wailing in the valley
of women losing a husband in the mines.

You will forget
the rough handshake of coarse palms
full of teary sorrow at the funeral.

If you stay in comfort too long
You will not hear
the shrieky voice of old warriors sing
the songs of fresh stored battlefields.

You will forget
the unfeeling bare feet
gripping the warm soil turned by the plough

You will forget
the voice of the season talking to the oxen.

Lost Bird

The migratory bird* flew with mirth,
his breast beating the air,
the wings waving like leaves.
He flew guided by the wind,
the warmth pulling his sensitive nose
And his choir
wrote a pattern in the sky.
But then disaster joined him,
A skirmish followed, nasty thing.
The bird dragged his breast over the city
compressed by smog.
His wings wagged, his heart beat
As he missed his airy path
over the smoke-laden city.
Some say he fell in the chimney

*The migratory bird is the harbinger of the rainy season in Shona.

of a nearby factory,
others say he choked
And fell in the sewerage works.
So he died, passed away without a tear.
And the children still stare
at the empty sky
with no season's song on their lips.**
That year the rains failed.
Then the sky had its share
of empty prayers, tasty meat for dogs.
Later, the bird's nest was empty:
so the secretary bird† roamed
the sky in uproarious song,
And women complained to their husbands,
Some nocturnal visitor
had castrated the women too,
So nobody would sing:
    Ngauzani Ngauzani.
    Ngauzani Ngauzani.‡

**The Shona have children's songs to celebrate the coming of the birds. The songs also celebrate nature's cyclic pattern.
†The secretary bird is evil when it roams the sky and roars like a bull. It is a sign of sure death or a number of deaths.
‡Children's song when they see the migratory birds. Children form a circle as they sing and run to the rhythm of the song.

Migratory Bird I*

One day he perched on a tree with dew
which is his heartbeat.
He had forgotten to drink;
for drink came only from eternity.
But his heart throbbed silently
and the rhythm of the seasons echoed in his heart.
Then he said, I will follow the seasons
either north or south.
Following the pangs of north, sought flight?
Neighbour eagle said, 'Why,
I stand still in the air
and defy the seasons'.
But he wouldn't hear,
for he had taken flight in obedience to the season's call.
Further on, his drenched wings weighed him down,
so he took to shelter:
Another season gone,
the migratory bird sings a rugged tune,
he can surely afford it
for the seasonal rhythm is in him,
and like repels like.

So we travel our several roads
Eagle on eagle-road perches
Migratory bird on season-road wings
And man on his lungs treads,
A new cannibal eating his own in a wage.

*When children see migratory birds going round and round in the sky, they sing songs of joy as they imitate the circular flight of the birds. This signifies a form of joining together with the birds, man and animal fused together in the circular motion of nature, of the seasons.

Child's Parliament

Mother sat
with hunger on her hands
and soaked love in her eyes.
Then the flies came
to sing nasty songs to her ears.
We listened to the interrupted tale
of hunger and strife.
But mother didn't sing
when singing time came
in the folk tale.
She just pointed to the flies
and asked us to hum
the same song sung by the wings.
We sang the winged song
as we joined the search.
Fly and child sang together
Mother and the leaves fell together,
father was not present,
and we never met him.
While the fly sings her search
we search together
Or form a joint committee
to resolve the issues of fly and child.
For on our hearts
are the steaming finger-prints of the fly
Whose wings told us stories
of the search for life, and to whom we belong.
Over the radio
we hear there is a crisis
members of Parliament demand higher salaries,
so there is no debate about us.
At least we are free from wrecked promises.
We shall debate

in the open chamber
with a thousand million diseases
standing for the Grave constituency.
And figures of population increase
standing for Survival constituency.
Dogs-cats-rats-fleas
send representatives to this chamber,
so the debate gets dreary at times.
Language problems!
lack of seats!
or simple lack of order in the house
Then we share all we have:-
from pocketfuls of blood
to parliamentary jargon.
Together we survive,
the subject of long debating sessions
and stale overdue projects
that crawl now
when they should have run yesterday.

The Other Syllabus

I had the lab science, the ecology of texts
and language of the pages.
I liked it all
as my joy spilled
with the test tube disasters
and the teacher's harmless roar
like a trapped mouse.
Then I left the lab,
Vomitted from the lab syllabus.
The streets, they had me also,
A scuffle followed: the other syllabus.
Bosses frowned
at my neat lab qualifications
only to declare them rubble.
Then I pocketed them,
now a wounded lion.
I crawled through streets,
streets that yawn in my face
like starved ghosts turned bitter.
Then a sick rat,
I gnawed at the remains
of this civilization that rots.
My comfort then lay in the rat-hole
where husband, wife, child, pot, fire,
mealie-meal
share the same mat,
and only mother's empty nipple
soothes the starved gums
of children who lie like discarded biltong
In this raid of slain dreams.

Country Life

Our hut puffs streaks of hope
in smoke that waves.
Inside, granny lies skeletal on the mat,
while her snuff-box dangles
in flashes of hope.
Her walking-stick waits
on stand-by
like the crafty workman.
Chicks may peck at her scars
and the wince tells floods of tales:
unless Takura comes to the rescue,
the hen calls for the whole invasion.

Outside, a path to the field
where little Tendai treads in bright song,
head flat aside
as the fields yawn in dismay
with the laziness of elders
who trudge along to the journey's end.

Look! mother's back is bare
as her babe lies in the shade
where lizards may lick if they will,
or ants drag if they may,
or birds drop their dung,
while mother pulls the hoe in deep song
as all is in mutinous harmony.

In the hills nearby,
a bell tinkles as the leaves rustle.
Farai lives this gong
which trickles down his moist heart
as the ox-bearer too grazes in nods,

nods that Farai lives by
together with the smell of torn grass,
veined leaves and fingered herbs
that unite man with the black soils of home.

Beyond and behind the hills,
clouds of dust swell,
raiding the air
and tearing the sky,
paving the way for man's soul.
Elderly throats bubble with elevated joy
that rides on *hungwe's* wings
while the drumming palms stretch in sinew.
Skins of drums loosen with beating
and man's soul swells out taut.
Bare soles patter the soil
to cement the relationship,
a slap of union in man and home.
Sand is ground to clay
which sinks under weight
to make a mat for tethered man,
as time will be
when these two shall (unashamedly)
kiss eternal loves.
Old men dance
with blood of usurped youth
and the young stare in disbelief
growing sky-bound
with decaying wishes.
Shiny bodies glitter in sweat
and damp voices drag along
in mysterious awe,
to reach the domes of survival within man,
where man hears not man
but only those that went before.

And now, down at the well
mother's soothe bathes the fields,
with the comfort of warmth
that the babe receives
in the pulse of mother's back.

Gabriel Gbadamosi

The Reading

In memory of my parents

I'm doing it again –
reading my father my new poems
in a trance-struck
adolescent voice.

Only this time
they're about my mother –
no-longer with him,
couched in her cold repose.

She peers over
the charmed boundary
from her corner
of our triangle,

to wonder am I alright
(her son, the poet)
and to squeeze my father's hand
so I don't notice.

Death Of The Polar Explorers

They made their grim, sad faces and went out,
Out into cold flurries of the snow, and ice,

And saw the glaciers perfecting time
In all their strange, enormous beauty. Doubt

Never stunned the marrow in their bones
Who passed beyond the merely physical –

And if they faltered it was only once,
On finding death incomprehensible.

from: Sango

Sango's son came down to the river.
The day was hot,
And a stranger accosted him.
Sango's voice is thunder
    in the stones of the river.
The stranger was Eshu,
    Eshu the deceiver,
Pretending to be human
As a man struggles to be human,
And finds only Death.
Death in the stones of the river.

Sango's son came down to the river.
The day was hot,
And a stranger accosted him.
Sango was king in Oyo, an Alafin,
    until strangers deposed him.
It is not easy to depose a king
Who has horses, and thunder in his face.
Sango entered the mountain,
His burial mound,
To strike fear into the hearts of strangers,
Strangers who oppose him.

Sango's son came down to the river.
The day was hot,
And a stranger accosted him.
Sango's son who is beautiful
    with the beauty of his father,
Who sleeps and rises from his mat
    knowing only the morning,
Who looks in the house, and on the road,
And finds nothing to inherit.
Nothing to inherit,
Except the strength his father has left him.

Sango's son came down to the river.
The day at its hottest,
A stranger accosted him.
Sango's arm is like the dam in the mountains.
The stranger was Eshu,
    Eshu the deceiver.
Sango's son found nothing to inherit,
And killed Eshu, the deceiver,
And took back what was his.
Death in the stones of the river.

BIOGRAPHICAL NOTES

Acholonu, Catherine Obianuju: Has published two volumes of poetry: *The Spring's Last Drop* (Owerri: Totan Publishers, 1985) and *Nigeria in the Year 1999* (Ibadan: Heinemann Educational Books, 1988), as well as plays and children's books. She currently teaches in the English Department at Alvan Ikoku College of Education, Owerri, Nigeria.

Awoonor, Kofi: Has published a much-acclaimed novel, *This Earth, My Brother* (New York: Doubleday, 1971); a study of African culture, *The Breast of the Earth* (New York: Doubleday, 1972); a book on Ewe traditional poetry, *Guardians of the Sacred Word* (New York: Nok Publications, 1974) and *Ghana: A Political History* (Accra: Woeli/SEDCO, 1990). Poetry: *Rediscovery* (Ibadan: Mbari, 1964); *Night of My Blood* (New York: Doubleday, 1971); *Ride Me, Memory* (New York: Greenfield Review Press, 1973); *The House By the Sea* (New York: Greenfield Press Review, 1978); and, *Until the Morning After: Collected Poems, 1963–1985* (New York: Greenfield Review Press, 1986). He won Dillons Commonwealth Poetry Prize (Africa) in 1989. He is currently Ghanaian Ambassador to Cuba.

Brutus, Dennis: One of South Africa's most highly-regarded poets. Poetry: *Sirens, Knuckles, Boots* (Ibadan: Mbari, 1963); *Letters to Martha, and other poems from a South African prison* (London: HEB, 1969); *Poems from Algiers* (Austin, Texas: African and Afro-American Research Institute, 1970); *China Poems* (Austin, Texas, 1970); *A Simple Lust* (London: HEB, 1973); *Strains* (Austin, Texas, 1975); *Stubborn Hope* (London: HEB, 1978). He lives in exile in the United States. He currently teaches at North-Western University, Chicago.

Cheney-Coker, Syl: His country's leading poet. Poetry: *Concerto for an Exile* (London: HEB, 1973); *The Graveyard also has Teeth*

(London: HEB, 1980); and *The Blood in the Desert's Eyes* (Oxford: Heinemann International, 1990). He lived for many years in Nigeria, where he taught at the University of Maiduguri. He now lives in Freetown, where he publishes a fortnightly newspaper, *The Vanguard*. He has also written a novel, *The Last Harmatten of Alusine Dunbar* (Oxford: Heinemann International, 1990), which won the African Commonwealth Writers Prize in 1991.

Chimombo, Steve: Has written plays and short stories and criticism. His volume of poetry, *Napolo Poems* (Zomba: Manchichi Publishers, 1987), received honourable mention in the 1988 Noma Award for publishing in Africa and he was nominated best first-time published poet, Africa Region, Commonwealth Poetry Competition, 1987. He is currently Associate Professor in English at Chancellor College, University of Malawi.

Chipasula, Frank: Has written radio plays and fiction. His volume of poetry, *O Earth, Wait for Me* (Johannesburg: Ravan Press, 1984) received Honourable Mention in the 1985 Noma Award for Publishing in Africa. Also: *Visions and Reflections* (Lusaka: National Educational Company of Zambia, 1972); *NIGHTWATCHER, Nightsong* (Peterborough: Paul Green, Dangerous Writers series, 1986); (editor) *When My Brothers Come Home: Poems from Central and Southern Africa* (Middletown, CT: Wesleyan University Press, 1985). He lives in the United States, where he is an Associate Professor in the Black Studies Department, University of Nebraska at Omaha.

Clark Bekederemo, J. P.: Well-known as a dramatist: *Three Plays* (London and New York: OUP, 1964); *Ozidi* (London and New York: OUP, 1966); and critic, *The Example of Shakespeare* (Harlow: Longman, 1970). Poetry: *Poems* (Ibadan: Mbari, 1962); *A Reed in the Tide* (Harlow: Longman, 1965); *Casualties: poems 1966/68* (Harlow: Longman, 1970); *A Decade of Tongues: Selected Poems, 1958–1968* (Harlow: Longman, 1981);

The State of the Union (Harlow: Longman, 1984); and, *Mandela and other poems* (Longman Nigeria, 1988). He was Professor of English at the University of Lagos for many years. He is currently Artistic Director of the PEC Repertory Theatre, Lagos.

Hove, Chenjerai: His novel, *Bones* (Harare: Baobab Books, 1988; Heinemann International AWS, 1989), won the 1988 Zimbabwean Publishers/Writers Literary Award, as well as the 1989 Noma Award. His volume of poetry, *Up in Arms* (Harare: Zimbabwe Publishing House, 1982), received Joint Special Commendation in the 1983 Noma Award for Publishing in Africa; another volume, *Red Hills of Home* (Gweru: Mambo Press, 1985), received Honourable Mention in the 1986 Noma Award. *Shadows* (Harare: Baobab Books, 1991; Heinemann International Literature and Textbooks, 1992) is his most recent novel. A former teacher, he is currently a cultural journalist based in Harare, Zimbabwe, and a contributor to *And Now The Poets Speak*.

Gbadamosi, Gabriel: His poems have been published in a variety of journals and magazines. Also a playwright, he was writer-in-residence at the Manchester Royal Exchange Theatre, 1988–1989, and the recipient of a Churchill Fellowship which enabled him to travel in West Africa to study drama.

Laing, Kojo: Has published three highly-acclaimed novels, *Search Sweet Country* (London: Wm Heinemann, 1986), *Woman of the Aeroplanes* (London: Wm Heinemann, 1988) and *Major Gentt and the Achimota Wars* (Heinemann Int. Lit. and Textbooks, 1992). Poetry: *God-horse* (Oxford: Heinemann International, 1989). He worked as Secretary to the Institute of African Studies at the University of Ghana until 1985, when he left to run a school in Accra.

Macgoye, Marjorie Oludhe: Although born in England, she moved to Kenya in 1954 and took out citizenship in 1964. She has published three novels: *Murder in Majengo* (Nairobi: OUP,

1972), *Coming to Birth* (London: Wm. Heinemann 1987; Kenya: Heinemann Kenya, 1987 and London: Virago, 1987) and *The Present Moment* (London: Wm. Heinemann and Heinemann Kenya, 1987). Poetry: *Song of Nyarloka and Other Poems* (Nairobi: OUP, 1977). A Novella: *Street Life* (Heinemann Kenya, 1988). She worked as an editor in Nairobi, Kenya, until she recently retired.

Mapanje, Jack: Has published one volume of poetry: *Of Chameleons and Gods* (London: HEB, 1981). Until his imprisonment, without charge or trial, in September, 1987, he was Head of the Department of English at Chancellor College, University of Malawi.

Mphande, Lupenga: His poems have been published in various journals. Worked as a literary critic of The Malawi Broadcasting Corporation until 1984. Currently Assistant Professor of African Languages and Literatures at the State University of Ohio at Columbus.

Nortje, Arthur: At the time of his death in 1970 from an overdose of drugs he was working for a doctorate at Jesus College, University of Oxford. His book, *Dead Roots* (London: HEB, 1973), was published posthumously.

Ofeimun, Odia: One of the most highly regarded of the Nigerian poets. Poetry: *The Poet Lied* (Harlow, Longman, 1981); *A Handle for the Flutist and other poems* (Lagos: Update Communications Ltd., 1986). He is presently a member of the editorial board of *The Guardian* (Lagos), and General Secretary of the Association of Nigerian Authors.

Ogundipe-Leslie, Molara: Well-known critic and social commentator. Poetry: *Sew the Old Days and other poems* (Ibadan: Evans, 1985). She is currently Professor and Head of the Department of English at Ogun State University, Nigeria.

Ojaide, Tanure: His collection, *Labyrinths of the Delta* (New York: Greenfield Review Press, 1986), was the Africa regional winner of the Commonwealth Poetry Prize for 1987. Also: *Children of Iroko and Other Poems* (New York: Greenfield Review Press, 1973); *The Endless Song* (1989); *The Eagle's Vision* (Detroit: Lotus, 1987); and, *The Fate of Vultures* (1989), the title poem of which was winner of the 1988 BBC Arts and Africa Poetry Award. He is currently a senior lecturer in Literature at the University of Maiduguri, Nigeria.

Okigbo, Christopher: Considered by many to be Nigeria's finest poet, he was killed fighting on the Biafran side in the early weeks of the civil war. He was 34 years old. Poetry: *Heavensgate* (Ibadan: Mbari, 1962); *Limits* (Ibadan: Mbari, 1964); *Labyrinths with Path of Thunder* (London: HEB, 1971); and *Christopher Okigbo: Collected Poems*, ed. Adewale Maja-Pearce (London: Wm. Heinemann, 1986).

Osundare, Niyi: His collection, *The Eye of the Earth* (Ibadan: HEB, 1986), was joint winner of the 1986 Commonwealth Poetry Prize. Also: *Songs of the Marketplace* (Ibadan: New Horn, 1983); *Village Voices* (Ibadan: Evans, 1984); *A Nib in the Pond* (Ile-Ife: Ife Monographs Series, 1986); *Moonsongs* (Ibadan: Spectrum Books, 1988), *Waiting Laughters* (Lagos: Malthouse Press, 1989) and *Selected Poems* (Heinemann Int. Lit. and Textbooks, 1992). He is currently a lecturer in English at the University of Ibadan, Nigeria.

Peters, Lenrie: Has published a novel, *The Second Round* (London: HEB, 1965). Poetry: *Poems* (Ibadan: Mbari, 1964); *Satellites* (London: HEB, 1967); *Katchikali* (London: HEB, 1971); and *Selected Poetry* (London: HEB, 1981). He practises as a surgeon in Banjul.

Soyinka, Wole: Better known as a dramatist. His plays include: *The Lion and the Jewel* (London and New York: OUP, 1963); *Kongi's Harvest* (London and New York: OUP, 1967); *Madmen and Specialists* (London: Methuen, 1971); *The Bacchae of*

Euripides (London: Methuen, 1973); *Opera Wonyosi* (London: Rex Collings, 1980); *Requiem for a Futurologist* (London: Rex Collings, 1985). He has also published a prison journal: *The Man Died* (London: Rex Collings, 1972); two novels, *The Interpreters* (London: André Deutsch, 1965; Heinemann Int. Lit. and Textbooks, 1970), and *Season of Anomy* (London: Rex Collings, 1973); and two volumes of autobiography, *Ake: The Years of Childhood* (London: Rex Collings, 1981) and *Isara: A Voyage around 'Essay'*. (London: Methuen, 1990). A substantial number of his essays have been collected in: *Art, Dialogue and Outrage: Essays on Literature and Culture* (Ibadan: New Horn, 1988). Poetry: *Idanre, and other poems* (London Methuen, 1967); *Poems from Prison* (London: Rex Collings, 1969); *A Shuttle in the Crypt* (London: Rex Collings, 1971); *Ogun Abibiman* (London: Rex Collings, 1976); *Mandela's Earth* (London: André Deutsch, 1988); edited, with an introduction: *Poems of Black Africa* (London: HEB, 1975). He was for many years Professor of Comparative Literature at Obafemi Awolowo University (formerly University of Ife), Nigeria. He was awarded the Nobel Prize for Literature in 1986.

Zimunya, Musaemura: Has published a book of criticism: *Those Years of Drought and Hunger: The Birth of African Fiction in English* (Gweru: Mambo Press, 1982). Two of his poetry collections, *Kingfisher, Jikinya, and other poems* (Harare: Longman Zimbabwe, 1982), and *Country Dawns and City Lights* (Harare: Longman Zimbabwe 1985), received 'Honourable Mention' in the 1983 and 1986 Noma Award for Publishing in Africa. Also: *Zimbabwe Ruins* (Harare: Poetry Society of Zimbabwe, 1979); *Thought Tracks* (London: Longman, 1982); co-editor, with M. Kadhani: *And Now the Poets Speak*; co-editor, with P. Porter and K. Anyidoho: *The Fate of Vultures* (Oxford: Heinemann, 1989); co-editor, with C. Hove and G. Mandishona: *Samora*, (Harare: Zimpapers, 1987); Editor *Birthright* (London: Longman, 1989). He is currently a lecturer in English at the University of Zimbabwe in Harare.

Some anthologies of African poetry

Messages: Poems from Ghana, edited by Kofi Awoonor and G. Adali–Mortty (London: HEB, 1971); *Poems from East Africa*, edited by David Cook and David Rubadari (London: HEB, 1971); *When Bullets Begin to Flower: Poems of Resistance from Angola, Mozambique and Guiné*, edited by Margaret Dickinson (Nairobi: East African Publishing House, 1972); *Black Poets in South Africa*, edited by Robert Royston (London: HEB, 1973); *Poems of Black Africa*, edited by Wole Soyinka (London: HEB, 1975); *Poets to the People: South African Freedom Poems*, edited by Barry Feinberg (London: HEB, 1980); *Summer Fires: New Poetry of Africa*, edited by Angus Calder, Jack Mapanje and Cosmo Pieterse (London: HEB, 1983); *The Penguin Book of Modern African Poetry*, edited by Gerald Moore and Ulli Beier (London: Penguin Books, Third edition, 1984); *The Heritage of African Poetry: An anthology of oral and written poetry*, edited with an introduction and notes by Isidore Okpewho (London: Longman, 1985); *When My Brothers Come Home: Poems from Central and Southern Africa*, edited by Frank Chipasula (Wesleyan University Press, 1985); *The Mambo Book of Zimbabwean Verse in English*, edited by Colin and O-lan Style (Harare: Mambo Press, 1986); *An Anthology of East African Poetry*, edited by A. D. Amateshe (London: Longman, 1988); *Boundless Voices: Poems from Kenya*, edited by Arthur I. Luvai (Nairobi: Heinemann Kenya, 1988); *Voices from the Fringe: An ANA Anthology of New Nigerian Poetry*, edited by Harry Garuba (Lagos: Malthouse Press, 1988); *The Fate of Vultures: New Poetry of Africa*, edited by Kofi Anyidoho, Peter Porter and Musaemura Zimunya (Oxford: Heinemann International, 1989); *The Penguin Book of Southern African Verse*, edited by Stephen Gray (London: Penguin Books, 1989).